Cooking Light

the ultimate
Kid-Approved
cookbook

Delicious Food Kids Will Eat, Nutritious Meals Moms Will Love

Cooking Light the ultimate Kid-Approved cookbook

Delicious Food Kids Will Eat, Nutritious Meals Moms Will Love

Oxmoor House®

This book is intended as a reference guide only but does not constitute
medical, nutritional, or other health-related advice. We strongly recommend that you consult with your child's pediatrician before modifying any
diet or eating regimen, or introducing new categories of food. If you have
any questions or concerns about your or your child's health, diet, eating
regimen, or food allergies, you should consult with a medical or health
professional.

To prevent choking, be sure food is cut into appropriately sized pieces,
particularly for young children. Foods most commonly associated with
choking include nuts, grapes, meat, carrots, apples, popcorn, hot dogs,
hard candy, and peanut butter.

ISBN-13: 978-0-8487-3453-4
ISBN-10: 0-8487-3453-X
Library of Congress Control Number: 2010940727
Printed in the United States of America
First Printing 2011

Oxmoor House
VP, Publishing Director: Jim Childs
Editorial Director: Susan Payne Dobbs
Brand Manager: Michelle Turner Aycock
Senior Editor: Heather Averett
Managing Editor: Laurie S. Herr

Cooking Light® *The Ultimate Kid-Approved Cookbook*
Editor: Rachel Quinlivan West, R.D.
Project Editor: Holly D. Smith
Senior Designer: Melissa Jones Clark
Assistant Designer: Allison L. Sperando
Director, Test Kitchens: Elizabeth Tyler Austin
Assistant Directors, Test Kitchens: Julie Christopher, Julie Gunter
Test Kitchens Professionals: Wendy Ball, Allison E. Cox, Victoria E. Cox,
    Margaret Monroe Dickey, Alyson Moreland Haynes, Stefanie Maloney,
    Callie Nash, Catherine Crowell Steele, Leah Van Deren
Photography Director: Jim Bathie
Senior Photo Stylist: Kay E. Clarke
Associate Photo Stylist: Katherine Eckert Coyne
Assistant Photo Stylist: Mary Louise Menendez
Senior Production Manager: Greg A. Amason

Contributors
Writer: Carolyn Land Williams, M.Ed., R.D.
Nutrition Editor: Caroline Glagola
Medical Consultant: Linda J. Stone, M.D.

Copy Editor: Julie Gillis
Proofreader: Dolores Hydock
Indexer: Mary Ann Laurens
Interns: Erin Bishop, Sarah H. Doss, Blair Gillespie, Alison Loughman,
    Rita A. Omokha, Lindsay A. Rozier, Caitlin Watzke
Test Kitchens Professional: Kathleen Royal Phillips
Photographers: Becky Luigart-Stayner, Mary Britton Senseney
Photo Stylists: Mindi Shapiro Levine, Leslie Simpson

Time Home Entertainment Inc.
Publisher: Richard Fraiman
General Manager: Steven Sandonato
Executive Director, Marketing Services: Carol Pittard
Executive Director, Retail & Special Sales: Tom Mifsud
Director, New Product Development: Peter Harper
Director, Bookazine Development & Marketing: Laura Adam
Assistant Director, Brand Marketing: Joy Butts
Associate Counsel: Helen Wan

Cooking Light®
Editor: Scott Mowbray
Creative Director: Carla Frank
Deputy Editor: Phillip Rhodes
Executive Editor, Food: Ann Taylor Pittman
Special Publications Editor: Mary Simpson Creel, M.S., R.D.
Senior Food Editor: Julianna Grimes
Associate Food Editor: Timothy Q. Cebula
Associate Editor: Cindy Hatcher
Assistant Editor: Phoebe Wu
Test Kitchens Director: Vanessa T. Pruett
Assistant Test Kitchens Director: Tiffany Vickers Davis
Recipe Testers and Developers: Robin Bashinsky, Adam Hickman,
    Deb Wise
Art Director: Fernande Bondarenko
Junior Deputy Art Director: Alexander Spacher
Associate Art Director: Rachel Lasserre
Designer: Chase Turberville
Photo Director: Kristen Schaefer
Senior Photographer: Randy Mayor
Senior Photo Stylist: Cindy Barr
Photo Stylist: Leigh Ann Ross
Chief Food Stylist: Charlotte Autry
Senior Food Stylist: Kellie Gerber Kelley
Copy Chief: Maria Parker Hopkins
Assistant Copy Chief: Susan Roberts
Research Editor: Michelle Gibson Daniels
Editorial Production Director: Liz Rhoades
Production Editor: Hazel R. Eddins
Art/Production Assistant: Josh Rutledge
Administrative Coordinator: Carol D. Johnson
CookingLight.com Editor: Allison Long Lowery
CookingLight.com Nutrition Editor: Holley Johnson Grainger, M.S., R.D.
Production Assistant: Mallory Daugherty

contents

welcome

Welcome to *The Ultimate Kid-Approved Cookbook*, a *Cooking Light* cookbook created to simplify family meals.

Do you struggle to prepare nutritious meals that everyone will eat? Are mealtimes often filled with drama over uneaten broccoli? Or do you feel like a short-order cook trying to please everyone? If so, you're not alone.

As a mother and a dietitian, I was determined to make family meals enjoyable and nutritious. After trying all sorts of games to get my daughter to eat, I decided on a different tactic: I started involving my 4-year-old in the cooking process. I gave Madeline small tasks to start with—pouring beans into a colander, sprinkling cheese on pizza, counting out potatoes—and it made her feel involved. She'd present the meal to the family and then eat up the black bean burritos and sautéed zucchini that she was so proud of preparing—and that she'd once claimed not to like.

Cooking with Madeline also started conversations about nutrition while in the kitchen. Right now, she likes to name as many vegetables as she can and then what colors they are, but I'm looking forward to a few years from now when we can actually plan meals together.

This book was designed to show you how to prepare quick, healthy meals that your kids will eat. Each of the more than 100 recipes in this book was reviewed by *Cooking Light's* dietitians and culinary professionals and then approved by our Kids Taste-Testing Panel. Each recipe also has suggestions for how kids of all ages can help in the kitchen. Getting kids involved not only makes them much more likely to try the dishes they helped prepare but also can initiate a lifelong interest in good nutrition and health.

Let *The Ultimate Kid-Approved Cookbook* help end the mealtime drama at your house and add fun around the table and in the kitchen with your family!

Happy meals,
Carolyn Land Williams, M.Ed., R.D.
Mom of Madeline, 4, and Griffin, 1

Raising Healthy Kids

Establishing good nutrition and active living habits for a lifetime

Nutrition for Growing Bodies

Every parent wants to see his or her child grow, thrive, and live a successful and productive life. To do this, we make sure our kids get the best education, encourage them to meet new friends and develop social skills, cheer on their competitive nature in sports, and try to feed them healthy diets for proper growth and development. We succeed at most of this, but when pressed for time, it's often the healthy diet that falls by the wayside.

The editors at *Cooking Light* (many of whom are parents) understand, and that's what prompted the development of this cookbook. Preparing quick, healthy meals that your kids will actually eat can be done! Use this cookbook to incorporate healthy foods into your family meals and to begin developing healthy family guidelines to keep your kids well nourished and fit for years to come.

The goal of this book is to help you do the following:

• Choose and prepare healthy meals for the whole family—even when pressed for time

• Incorporate kids in the cooking and meal-planning process

• Establish healthy eating and activity habits to last a lifetime

Nutrients Kids Need

Nutrients are what give us energy, help us grow, and keep our hearts beating and our body systems running efficiently. Because children are constantly growing, consuming a nutrient-rich diet is essential. There are six groups of nutrients:

Carbohydrates

• The body's main source of energy and fuel

• Found in grains, vegetables, fruits, beans, and dairy foods, as well as added sugars

• Include fiber that keeps our digestive systems running smoothly

Proteins

• Essential for building and maintaining the body

• Found in meats, seafood, beans, nuts, and dairy foods

Fats

• Vital for keeping skin, hair, and nails healthy and for absorbing vitamins

• Some body fat is needed to protect organs and to insulate the body

Vitamins

• Each food has a unique assortment of vitamins

• Grains and protein foods are rich in B vitamins; fortified dairy foods are rich in vitamin D; vegetables and fruits are rich in vitamin A and C; plant oils and nuts are rich in vitamin E

Minerals

• Each food has its own assortment of minerals

• Two important minerals for growing kids are iron (found in protein foods, whole grains, and some vegetables) and calcium (found in dairy foods and some vegetables)

Water

• Makes up more than half of our body weight and must be replaced daily

Nutrients and the Food Groups

Each food that kids eat gives them a different assortment of the six nutrients listed above, which is why it's so important for them to eat a variety of foods. The USDA has placed foods into groups because they have similar nutrients. For example, foods in the milk group, such as yogurt, cheese, and milk, are all good sources of protein, calcium, and vitamin D. Eating foods from each group every day provides most of the nutrients that kids need.

grains ⊹ vegetables ⊹ fruit ⊹ dairy ⊹ protein foods ⊹ fats & oils

grains group

There are two types of grains: whole grains and refined grains. Refined grains have had the outer parts of the grain kernel removed, a process that strips the grain of nutrients. Whole grains are the best choice because they contain more fiber, vitamins, and minerals. Both kids and adults should aim for *at least* half of their daily servings to be from whole-grain sources (see Best Choices).

nutrients: Carbohydrates, fiber*, B vitamins (thiamin, riboflavin, niacin, folate), iron*, magnesium*, selenium*
Greater sources of these nutrients are found in whole grains. **servings:** Approximately 4-5 ounces for kids and 6-8 ounces for adults

best choices:

1 ounce of whole grains or whole-grain products

1 ounce is equivalent to:
* 1 slice whole-wheat bread
* 1 small corn or whole-wheat tortilla
* ½ cup cooked oatmeal, brown rice, wild rice, or whole-wheat pasta
* 1 whole-wheat bun, roll, or mini bagel
* ½ whole-wheat English muffin or pita
* 1 cup whole-grain breakfast cereal (with no added sugar or fat)
* 5 whole-wheat crackers or 3 cups fat-free or air-popped popcorn
* 1 whole-wheat or buckwheat pancake

ok choices:

1 ounce of refined grain products

1 ounce is equivalent to:
* 1 slice white or wheat bread
* 1 small corn or flour tortilla
* ½ cup white rice, pasta, or grits
* 1 package instant flavored oatmeal
* 1 bun, roll, small low-fat muffin, mini bagel, or pancake
* ½ English muffin or pita
* 1 cup breakfast cereal with a moderate amount of added sugar and fat (less than 10g of sugar and less than 3g of fat)
* 5 low-fat crackers or 15 pretzels

limit:

Refined grain products with added fat and/or added sugar such as doughnuts, muffins, croissants, garlic bread, crackers, snack foods, and refined pastas

vegetable group

The vegetable group is where you find many of nature's healthiest foods. Vegetables are full of fiber, vitamins, and minerals and are low in calories, fat, sodium, and cholesterol. Vegetables are divided into five subgroups based on nutrient content—dark-green vegetables, orange vegetables, beans and peas, starchy vegetables, and a group for all others. Serve your child a variety of vegetables from all the subgroups each week.

nutrients: Fiber and abundant vitamins and minerals, which vary by vegetable **servings:** Approximately 1½ to 2 cups for kids and 2 to 3 cups for adults

best choices:

fresh or frozen vegetables
1 cup of vegetables is equivalent to:
1 cup cooked **or** 2 cups raw
- **Dark-green:** spinach, broccoli, greens (collard, mustard), romaine, bok choy
- **Orange:** Butternut and acorn squash, pumpkin, sweet potatoes, carrots
- **Beans and peas:** black, garbanzo, navy, soy and soybean products (like tofu), kidney, black-eyed peas, lentils
- **Starchy:** potatoes, peas, corn
- **Other:** onions, tomatoes, zucchini, summer squash, celery, cucumbers, cabbage

ok choices:
- Canned vegetables, due to the high amount of sodium
- Vegetables in a low-fat sauce

limit:
Fried vegetables such as French fries and vegetables in butter, cream, or cheese sauces

fruit group

Naturally sweet and juicy, fruits are also low in calories, fat, sodium, and cholesterol and are bursting with an array of vitamins and minerals. Fruit may already be a staple in your house, so if that's the case, keep it up! Remember to introduce kids to all types of fruit because each offers its own assortment of nutrients. And try to choose whole fruit or cut-up fruit over fruit juices to get more fiber and fewer calories per serving. Be sure to cut fruit into appropriately sized pieces for younger children.

nutrients: Carbohydrates, fiber, folate, vitamin C, potassium **servings:** Approximately 1 to 1½ cups for kids and 1½ to 2 cups for adults

best choices:

All fresh fruits, fruits canned in water, frozen fruits, and unsweetened fruit purees
½ cup of fruit is equivalent to:
- 1 small apple, small orange, small peach, large plum, or small banana
- ½ cup sliced strawberries, chopped apple, or chopped pineapple
- 1 snack container of unsweetened applesauce, mixed fruit in juice, or other fruit in juice
- 6 melon balls

ok choices:

All unsweetened dried fruits and 100% fruit juice
½ cup of fruit is equivalent to:
- 1 small box raisins
- ¼ cup dried fruit
- ½ cup of 100% fruit juice

limit:

Fruit punches, drinks, and juices with added sugars; fruits canned or frozen in syrup; and sweetened purees such as sweetened applesauce

dairy group

Milk has long been a mealtime staple for kids. Full of bone-building calcium and vitamin D, milk and dairy foods offer a mix of protein, carbohydrates, B vitamins, and potassium. Early in life most kids need the extra fat provided in whole or 2% milk for growth. But after children reach the age of 2, the American Academy of Pediatrics recommends they be weaned from higher-fat milks (2% and whole) unless directed otherwise by your pediatrician. If your child still loves whole milk, then start by slowly stepping him down to 2% and then to 1% or fat-free milk and dairy products.

nutrients: Protein, calcium, vitamin D, potassium  **servings:** Approximately 2 to 3 cups for kids and adults

best choices:

All fat-free or low-fat (1% milk fat) milks, yogurts, and cheeses with no added sugar

1 cup in the milk and dairy group is equivalent to:

* 1 cup (8 ounces) milk
* 1 cup or 1 (8-ounce) carton of plain yogurt or flavored yogurt sweetened with low-calorie sweetener
* 2 cups cottage cheese
* ⅓ cup shredded cheese
* 1 cheese stick
* 1½ ounces hard cheese (Parmesan, cheddar, Swiss, etc.)
* 1 cup pudding made with fat-free milk and sweetened with low-calorie sweetener

ok choices:

All fat-free or low-fat (1% milk fat) milks, yogurts, and cheeses with added sugar

1 cup in the milk and dairy group is equivalent to:

* 1 cup (8 ounces) chocolate milk
* 1 cup or 1 (8-ounce) carton of flavored yogurt
* 1 cup pudding or low-fat frozen yogurt

limit:

Full-fat milks, cheeses, yogurts, and dairy-based desserts such as ice cream

protein foods group

This group is the primary source of protein in the diet. Protein is the most satiating nutrient—meaning it makes you feel full and content longer—so it is good to incorporate a little protein into each meal and snack to help keep energy levels up. Recent recommendations encourage everyone to choose leaner sources of protein, such as seafood, beans, soy products, and lean meats and poultry.

nutrients: Protein, vitamin B6, vitamin B12, iron, zinc, magnesium **servings:** Approximately 3 to 5 ounces for kids and 5 to 6½ ounces for adults

best choices:

1 ounce of meat or beans is equivalent to:
- 1 ounce cooked fish and shellfish
- Approximately ¼ cup drained canned fish
- ¼ cup cooked beans
- 2 tablespoons hummus
- 1 tablespoon peanut butter or nut butter
- ¼ cup cooked tofu
- ½ ounce nuts and seeds (approximately 12 almonds or 7 walnut halves)

ok choices:

1 ounce of meat or beans is equivalent to:
- 1 ounce cooked skinless chicken or turkey
- 1 ounce cooked lean ground meat or poultry
- 1 egg
- 1 ounce cooked lean, trimmed cuts of beef, pork, ham, or lamb

limit:

High-fat meats, meat and poultry with skin, canned fish and shellfish in oil, fried meat, fried poultry, and fried seafood

fat & oil group

Fat is naturally found in some foods, and fat may also be added to food during cooking or manufacturing. However, different fats have different effects on the body—some good and some bad. The healthy fats are unsaturated fats found in most vegetable oils, nuts, avocados, and fatty fish such as salmon. These fats protect our hearts and are the ones we should choose most often. The unhealthy fats are saturated fats (found in animal foods such as ground beef or whole milk) and trans fats (found predominantly in snack foods, baked goods, and fried foods). By choosing low-fat food items that aren't processed or fried, you can avoid most unhealthy fats.

nutrients: Vitamin E and essential fatty acids **servings:** Approximately 4 to 5 teaspoons for kids and 5 to 7 teaspoons for adults

best choices:

1 teaspoon of oil is equivalent to:
- 1 teaspoon of plant-based cooking oil (canola, olive, corn, peanut, safflower, soybean)
- 8 olives
- ¼ of an avocado or 1 slice avocado
- 1 tablespoon oil-based salad dressing such as Italian
- 2 tablespoons reduced-fat oil-based salad dressing
- 4-5 tree nuts including almonds, walnuts, and pecans

ok choices:

1 teaspoon of oil is equivalent to:
- 2 tablespoons light or reduced-fat mayonnaise or creamy oil-based salad dressing such as ranch
- 1 tablespoon margarine (made with no trans fats)

limit:

Full-fat mayonnaise, salad dressings, and solid fats—such as butter, lard, and shortening—bacon, hydrogenated oils, and fried foods

extras

There are many foods you can think of that may not "fit" into one of the food groups. Many of these foods are what we may call "extras" and include sugary sweets such as birthday cake, lollipops, and sugary beverages such as sodas. These foods aren't included in a food group because they provide few nutrients, lots of added sugar, and sometimes added fat. Although these foods should be limited, there are ways to incorporate them into your child's diet. There are also healthier alternatives to each that at times may be just as appealing to your child.

nutrients: Limited **servings:** Less than 5 per week

limit:
Lemonade, fruit punch, sodas, and sugary beverages

alternatives:
- 100% fruit juice or fruit-flavored water

limit:
Ice cream and frozen treats

alternatives:
- Low-fat frozen yogurt
- Sugar-free gelatin
- Frozen grapes
- Pudding made with fat-free milk and low-calorie sweetener
- Smoothies made with fresh fruit and low-fat yogurt

limit:
Cookies, candy, and other sweets

alternatives:
- Homemade trail mix with whole-grain cereal, pretzels, nuts, dried fruit
- Low-fat chocolate milk
- Peanut butter on graham crackers
- Popcorn sprinkled with cinnamon-sugar

Meal Plans

We've included daily serving recommendations from each food group based on age and children's approximate calorie needs. Some children may need slightly more or less calories according to growth and physical activity. Your pediatrician can assess your child's weight and height, identify any specific nutrition needs, and further tailor this plan to fit those needs. Visit ChooseMyPlate.gov to get a plan specifically for your child.

daily serving recommendations

Preschoolers (ages 3-5 yrs):

Grains: 4 ounces
Vegetables: 1½ cups
Fruits: 1½ cups
Milk: 2 cups
Meats and beans: 3 ounces
Oils: 4 teaspoons
Extras: 170 calories
Activity: At least 60 minutes

Young Children (ages 6-8 yrs):

Grains: 5 ounces
Vegetables: 1½ cups
Fruits: 1½ cups
Milk: 2 cups
Meats and beans: 4 ounces
Oils: 4 teaspoons
Extras: 170 calories
Activity: At least 60 minutes

Older Children (ages 9-12 yrs):

Grains: 5 ounces
Vegetables: 2 cups
Fruits: 1½ cups
Milk: 3 cups

Meats and beans: 5 ounces
Oils: 5 teaspoons
Extras: 130 calories
Activity: At least 60 minutes

*All plans are from ChooseMyPlate.gov and are based on average calorie needs for children within the specified age ranges.

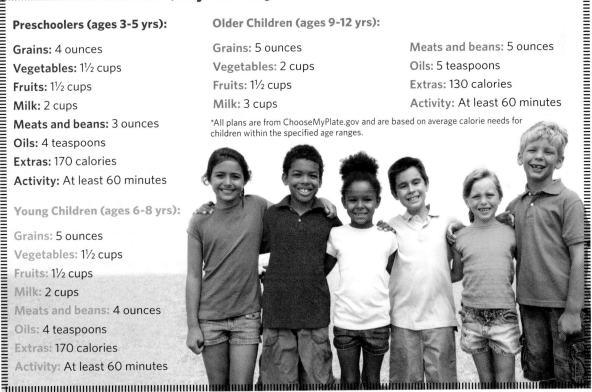

Physical Activity

Making healthy food choices is only part of a healthy lifestyle. The other component is being physically active. This doesn't mean your child has to hit the treadmill, though; lots of games and playtime activities count as physical activity. Below are suggestions on how to make everyday activities fun, as well as activity ideas by age group.

How much is needed?

Children need **at least** 60 minutes of moderate to vigorous activity each day. Here are a few tips for making it more doable:

Choose fun, age-appropriate activities. Conventional group activities (soccer, football, basketball), individual activities (bike riding, walking, ballet, skateboarding), as well as creative play activities (dancing to favorite songs, playing tag) all count. The definition of "fun" will depend largely on your child's age, so make sure activities are engaging and challenging, yet age-appropriate.

Be creative! Add an element of fun, learning, or play to regular mundane activities, and time literally flies. For example, sing the "Alphabet Song" or play "I Spy" on walks; count the number of cats you see while rollerblading; or make the number of laps, blocks, or miles you cover on a bike ride part of a giant math equation. For older kids, have a family-activity challenge where each family member commits to a certain physical activity at the start of the week. Celebrate those family members who succeed in doing the activity they committed to with a special movie or family event, like bowling.

Why Kids Need Activity

Benefits of Being Active

Kids who get regular physical activity:

- Have stronger bones, muscles, cardiovascular systems, and endurance
- Have higher self-esteem and confidence
- Often make better grades in school
- Sleep better
- Are less likely to become overweight
- Are less likely to develop type 2 diabetes or hypertension

Preschoolers:

- Bike riding or scooter riding
- Skipping
- Duck, duck, goose
- London bridge
- Playing on swing sets and playgrounds
- Dancing to kids' music
- Doing the Hokey Pokey

Early Elementary:

- Bike riding or scooter riding
- Hide-and-seek
- Playing tag
- Hopscotch
- Jump rope
- Organized sports like soccer, flag football, and kickball
- Individual sports like ballet, swimming, and karate
- P.E. class

Late Elementary/Preteen:

- Bike riding or scooter riding
- Organized sports like soccer, flag football, and kickball
- Individual sports like ballet, swimming, and karate
- Walking and running
- Skateboarding and rollerblading
- Scavenger hunts
- P.E. class

Get Kids Involved

Kids are eager to learn and to get involved, and everyday tasks such as grocery shopping that may seem mundane to parents can be great learning opportunities. Here are 12 easy ways to teach kids about nutrition and activity and to encourage healthy lifestyle habits.

Be a role model.

The **best way** to teach children healthy habits is to practice healthy habits. Even though you may think your kids are not paying attention, they watch everything that you do and will eventually adopt the behaviors that they see. By eating healthy and being active, you're sending a powerful message to your children.

Go shopping.

The grocery store is a classroom for all ages! Younger kids can identify colors and practice counting skills in the produce section; older kids can practice reading skills and learn to read labels. Let children pick a new fruit, vegetable, or herb to try. If they're involved, they will be much more likely to try a new food.

Explore new foods.

The more foods you introduce to children, the greater the variety of foods they will eat as adults. Preparing ethnic dishes offers a great opportunity to try new foods, flavors, and spices, as well as to learn about a new culture. Consider having a theme night, complete with music from that culture. Older kids can research that part of the world and share fun facts at dinner.

Plan meals together.

Part of eating a healthy diet is pairing foods together to get a variety of nutrients. Let older children help plan meals using the food guides on page 19. Challenge your child to help you plan a meal with one whole grain, two vegetables, and three ounces of meat. For younger children, let them help you choose a plate full of colors (red strawberries, green broccoli, yellow corn, and brown chicken).

Get cooking.

Involve your child in the cooking process. Though it does require a little patience and time, cooking with your child offers many opportunities to learn and to bond, as well as to establish a lifelong interest in food and nutrition.

Make mealtime a happy time.

Create a relaxed meal environment by turning off cell phones and televisions. Avoid food fights by never pressuring your child to try something or to clean his plate; simply offer what has been prepared and let him take it or leave it. Discourage negative comments about foods being served.

Eat as a family.

Kids like routines, and regular meals eaten as a family provide needed structure and reassurance. Family meals are also a perfect opportunity to talk about events from the day and to reconnect as a family. Some research has even suggested that children who eat regular family meals are less likely to be overweight.

Start a garden.

Gardening helps kids understand the full circle of life, teaches responsibility, and provides daily physical activity. If you don't have a green thumb, start with a pot of herbs, such as rosemary or basil. Your child will enjoy watching them grow, and then picking and cooking with the herbs.

Be active together.

Going on walks after dinner or bike rides on the weekends allows everyone to get exercise. It also provides family time to catch up and bond.

Take field trips.

Visit a farmers' market, talk to the farmers about how they grow food, and let your child pick out fresh fruits and vegetables. Tours of local dairies and farms also make great outings for kids to learn about food and where it comes from.

Consider a screen time limit.

It's hard to leave video games, computers, and TVs, but these sedentary activities are contributing factors to the growing obesity crisis. As a parent, look closely at how much time your child spends being sedentary versus being active, and consider a time limit such as 60 minutes of screen time per day.

Schedule and plan in advance.

Just like adults, kids are busy people, so start a family activity calendar. Prior to the start of each week, let each family member pencil in when and how they plan to be physically active.

Kids in the Kitchen

Involving your kids in the cooking process can be fun for both parent and child. Cooking is also a great opportunity to reinforce skills learned in school and to build self-confidence, as well as to bond with your child.

How To Use This Book

The Ultimate Kid-Approved Cookbook is designed for both parents and children to use together. The task lists for younger and older chefs are meant to serve as a *general* guide for parents to incorporate their children into the cooking process. Because every child is unique, parents should adapt these tasks based on a child's age, development, and capabilities. Within each chapter you will find the following:

Nutrition Notes: Answers and solutions to common nutrition questions and concerns about kids for parents

Meals Made Easy: Quick sides to round out recipes and create a balanced meal or snack

Kitchen Classroom: Kid-friendly lessons on the science, history, or math behind a recipe or cooking technique

Tasks for Younger Chefs: Tasks within a recipe that most children between the ages of 3 to 6 years can do

Tasks for Older Chefs: Tasks within a recipe that most children between the ages of 7 to 12 years can do

Kid-Approved: Comments and thoughts about the recipes from our Kids Taste-Testing Panel

Guidelines for Cooking with Kids

Clean

• Always wash hands before starting to cook and after touching raw meat, poultry, or seafood.

• Clean up as you cook, making it part of the process.

• Don't mix raw and cooked foods.

• Clean cutting boards and counters that raw meat, poultry, or seafood has touched, or have cutting boards with different colors to identify one for meat and one for fruits and vegetables.

Prepare

• Set kitchen rules, and communicate those clearly. Read each recipe before beginning, and have your child read it if he or she is able.

• Locate ingredients and equipment, and chop or measure as needed before starting.

• Create a small, safe workplace in the kitchen for younger children, and provide plenty of kid-friendly utensils.

Don't Assume

• Never assume children will know what to do by watching—explain as you go, demonstrate, and then let them try.

• Kids don't necessarily know that an object or utensil may be hot or sharp, so make sure to tell them and to set rules about usage.

Prevent

• Keep sharp or dangerous items, such as knives, scissors, and food processors, out of reach.

• Clean up spills as they happen.

• Don't sample food until it's done.

Supervise

• Always supervise children in the kitchen.

• For older children, identify what is and isn't OK to do when you're not in the kitchen.

Why Cook with Kids

The benefits of cooking with your child include:

• Increased self-confidence for your child
• Practice working as a team
• Development of fine motor skills
• Color identification and counting skills
• Greater likelihood to try the foods prepared
• Better understanding of nutrition
• Reading and comprehension
• Math skills

Note to Readers: This book includes activities for both younger chefs and older chefs and suggests fun recipes that families can enjoy together. Of course, keep in mind that skill levels may vary. Children should be supervised by a responsible adult at all times while performing the activities mentioned in this book. The editors and publisher of this book do not assume any responsibility or liability for any injuries, damages, or losses that may be incurred while performing these activities.

Breakfast

Fueling little bodies for the day

Breakfast

We know you've heard it before, but breakfast really is the most important meal of the day—especially for your child. Studies suggest that children who eat breakfast are more attentive and perform better in school. A healthy breakfast contains a mix of complex carbohydrates and protein to fuel your little one until he eats again. Try pairing whole grains such as oatmeal, whole-wheat toast, or whole-grain cereal with a protein source such as milk, yogurt, peanut butter, eggs, or cheese. Add in a side of fruit for a boost of vitamins and minerals, and your child is ready for the day.

Banana Breakfast Smoothie

Freezing banana slices the night before makes this creamy beverage extra thick and cold. The smoothie can be served alone or paired with a handful of whole-grain dry cereal or a granola bar for a filling breakfast.

Young Chefs can:

• Peel banana
• Pour ingredients into blender with assistance

Older Chefs can:

▪ Help slice banana with dinner knife
▪ Push buttons to process ingredients

½ cup 1% low-fat milk
½ cup crushed ice
1 tablespoon honey
1 large ripe banana, sliced and frozen
1 (6-ounce) carton vanilla fat-free yogurt

1. Place first 4 ingredients in a blender; process 1 minute or until smooth. Add yogurt; process 20 to 30 seconds or until blended. Serve immediately.
Yield: 2 servings (serving size: 1 cup).

CALORIES 151; FAT 0.6g (sat 0.4g, mono 0.2g, poly 0g); PROTEIN 5.2g; CARB 32.9g; FIBER 1.4g; CHOL 5mg; IRON 0.2mg; SODIUM 78mg; CALC 206mg

 meals made easy

Banana Breakfast Smoothie + + peanut or almond butter

Blackberry-Mango Breakfast Shake

Silken tofu gives this drink a smooth, creamy consistency. If you don't like the seeds in blackberries, substitute frozen blueberries.

Young Chefs can:

- Place blackberries in measuring cups
- Pour ingredients into blender with assistance

Older Chefs can:

- Drain mango slices
- Measure ingredients
- Push buttons to process ingredients

1	cup orange juice
1	cup refrigerated bottled mango slices
¾	cup light firm silken tofu
3	tablespoons honey
1½	cups frozen blackberries

1. Place all ingredients in a blender in the order given; process until smooth. **Yield:** 4 servings (serving size: about 1 cup).

CALORIES 162; FAT 0.6g (sat 0.1g, mono 0.1g, poly 0.3g); PROTEIN 3.7g; CARB 38.3g; FIBER 3.5g; CHOL 0mg; IRON 1mg; SODIUM 45mg; CALC 34mg

Wholesome Granola + +

Wholesome Granola

Flaxseed is a great source of omega-3 fatty acids, which are essential for brain development and heart health. Serve in a bowl with milk, as a topping for yogurt or oatmeal, or as a snack by itself.

Young Chefs can:

• Measure nuts and raisins
• Combine dry ingredients

Older Chefs can:

• Line pan with foil
• Combine ingredients in saucepan
• Stir in raisins

2   cups old-fashioned rolled oats
1/3   cup flaxseed meal
1/4   cup chopped walnuts
1/4   cup chopped slivered almonds
1 1/2 teaspoons ground cinnamon
1/3   cup orange juice
1/3   cup honey
1/4   cup packed light brown sugar
2   teaspoons vegetable oil
1   teaspoon vanilla extract
Cooking spray
1/3   cup raisins

1. Preheat oven to 300°. **2. Combine** first 5 ingredients in a medium bowl. **3. Combine** orange juice, honey, and brown sugar in a small saucepan. Cook

nutrition note

Old-Fashioned vs. Instant Oats

Old-fashioned rolled oats is what most of us know as oatmeal. It's made from whole groats that have been steamed and flattened by large rollers. They cook in about 5 minutes. Instant oats are regular rolled oats that have been flattened even more, then cooked and dried. Instant oats are not the same as the sugary pulverized oats in individual packets.

over medium heat just until sugar dissolves, stirring constantly. Remove from heat; stir in oil and vanilla. **4. Pour** honey mixture over oat mixture, stirring to coat. Spread mixture in a thin layer onto a foil-lined jelly-roll pan coated with cooking spray. Bake at 300° for 10 minutes; stir. Bake an additional 15 minutes or until golden brown. Spoon granola into a bowl; stir in raisins. Let cool completely. Store in an airtight container. **Yield:** 8 servings (serving size: 1/2 cup). **Note:** Store completely cooled granola in an airtight container at room temperature for up to 2 weeks.

CALORIES 243; FAT 8.5g (sat 0.7g, mono 2.7g, poly 4.3g); PROTEIN 5.1g; CARB 40.5g; FIBER 4.5g; CHOL 0mg; IRON 1.6mg; SODIUM 3mg; CALC 35mg

Overnight Honey-Almond Oatmeal

Steel-cut oats soak up water overnight so they're ready to cook quickly on busy school mornings. Using a big bowl allows room for the grains to expand.

Young Chefs can:

- Help measure oats
- Sprinkle oatmeal with almonds

Older Chefs can:

- Combine first three ingredients
- Stir in honey and spices

1¼	cups water
⅓	cup steel-cut oats
2	tablespoons uncooked pearl barley
⅛	teaspoon salt
1	tablespoon honey
¼	teaspoon ground cinnamon
⅛	teaspoon ground nutmeg
1	tablespoon sliced almonds, toasted
1	tablespoon turbinado sugar (optional)
1	tablespoon honey (optional)

1. Combine first 3 ingredients in a 1-quart microwave-safe bowl. Cover and refrigerate 4 hours or overnight.
2. Uncover bowl, and stir in salt. Microwave, uncovered, at HIGH 6 minutes or until most of liquid is absorbed, stirring well after 3 minutes. Stir in honey, cinnamon, and nutmeg. Spoon evenly into 2 bowls. Top with almonds. If desired, sprinkle evenly with turbinado sugar or drizzle with 1 tablespoon honey.
Yield: 2 servings (serving size: ½ cup cereal and 1½ teaspoons almonds).

CALORIES 144; FAT 2.5g (sat 0.3g, mono 1.3g, poly 0.8g); PROTEIN 3.6g; CARB 28.3g; FIBER 3.9g; CHOL 0mg; IRON 1.1mg; SODIUM 153mg; CALC 20mg

nutrition note

How to Pick a Healthy Breakfast Cereal

With boxes touting "made with whole grains," "less sugar," and "good source of fiber," one would assume that most cereals are a nutritious breakfast option. But the truth is that labels can be deceiving. Just because a cereal states it has "whole grains" doesn't mean it's necessarily a good choice. So how do you pick a nutritious cereal? Do your own cereal detective work by following these two easy tips.

❶ **Check out the Nutrition Facts panel.** Try to choose a cereal that has all of the following:

- less than 3 grams of fat per serving
- at least 3 grams of protein per serving
- at least 3 grams of fiber per serving

❷ **Check out the ingredient list** (usually located below the Nutrition Facts). You want whole grains like whole-wheat flour, oats, rye, or barley to be among the first few ingredients listed. Also, look for cereals made with little or no added sugars. Any sweeteners, such as brown sugar, honey, and corn syrup, should be toward the end of the list.

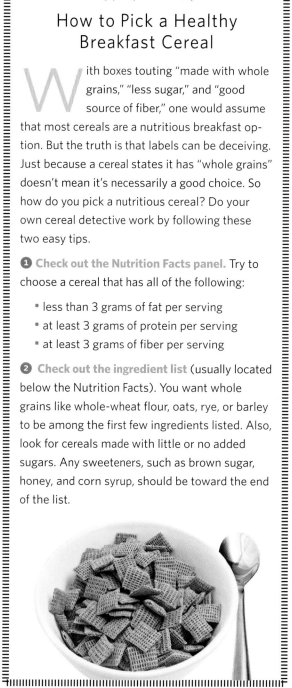

Blueberry Power Muffins ÷ ÷ **fat-free or 1% low-fat milk**

Blueberry Power Muffins

We call these "power" muffins because they're loaded with B vitamins from whole-wheat flour, calcium from milk and yogurt, antioxidants from blueberries, and heart-friendly monounsaturated fat from almonds and canola oil. You can freeze these muffins for up to a month, then thaw them at room temperature, or microwave each frozen muffin at HIGH 15 to 20 seconds.

Young Chefs can:

- Measure blueberries and add to batter
- Sprinkle streusel over batter

Older Chefs can:

- Combine dry ingredients
- Help spoon batter into muffin cups

MUFFINS:

6.75 ounces all-purpose flour (about 1½ cups)

4.8 ounces whole-wheat flour (about 1 cup)

1 cup quick-cooking oats

1 cup granulated sugar

1 tablespoon baking powder

1 teaspoon baking soda

¼ teaspoon salt

2 cups vanilla low-fat yogurt

½ cup 2% reduced-fat milk

3 tablespoons canola oil

2 teaspoons vanilla extract

1 large egg

1½ cups blueberries

Cooking spray

STREUSEL:

1.1 ounces all-purpose flour (about ¼ cup)

¼ cup slivered almonds, chopped

1 tablespoon brown sugar

1 tablespoon butter, melted

1. Preheat oven to 400°. **2. To prepare muffins,** weigh or lightly spoon flours into dry measuring cups; level with a knife. Combine flours, oats, and next 4 ingredients in a large bowl, stirring with a whisk. Make a well in center of mixture. Combine yogurt and next 4 ingredients, stirring with a whisk. Add yogurt mixture to flour mixture, stirring just until moist. Fold in blueberries. Spoon batter into 24 muffin cups coated with cooking spray, filling two-thirds full. **3. To prepare streusel,** weigh or lightly spoon flour into a dry measuring cup; level with a knife. Combine flour and next 3 ingredients, stirring until crumbly. Sprinkle streusel evenly over batter. **4. Bake** at 400° for 15 minutes or until muffins spring back when touched lightly in center. Cool in pans 10 minutes on a wire rack; remove from pans. Serve warm or at room temperature. **Yield:** 24 servings (serving size: 1 muffin).

CALORIES 157; FAT 3.8g (sat 0.8g, mono 1.7g, poly 0.8g); PROTEIN 3.6g; CARB 27.7g; FIBER 1.6g; CHOL 12mg; IRON 1mg; SODIUM 148mg; CALC 72mg

Ham and Cheese Breakfast Sandwich

This sandwich packs protein from egg, calcium from cheese, and fiber and B vitamins from the whole-wheat muffin. For a touch of sweetness, spread your favorite jelly or jam over the bottom half of each sandwich.

Young Chefs can:

- Place muffin halves on baking sheet
- Sprinkle cheese on muffins

Older Chefs can:

- Coat pan with cooking spray
- Assemble sandwiches

Cooking spray

4   ($\frac{1}{2}$-ounce) slices Canadian bacon

4   large eggs

4   whole-wheat English muffins, split and toasted

$\frac{3}{4}$ cup (3 ounces) reduced-fat shredded extrasharp cheddar cheese

1. Preheat broiler. **2. Heat** a large nonstick skillet over medium-high heat. Coat pan with cooking spray. Add bacon; cook 2 minutes on each side or until lightly browned. Remove from pan; keep warm. Reduce heat to medium; recoat pan with cooking spray. Break eggs into hot pan; cook 1 minute on each side or until desired degree of doneness. **3. Place** muffin halves, cut sides up, on a baking sheet. Top with 1 bacon slice, 1 egg, and 1 tablespoon cheese. Sprinkle 2 tablespoons cheese over top half of each muffin. Broil 1$\frac{1}{2}$ minutes or until bubbly. Place top halves of muffins over bottom halves. **Yield:** 4 servings (serving size: 1 sandwich).

CALORIES 283; FAT 11.7g (sat 4.9g, mono 2.4g, poly 0.8g); PROTEIN 20.5g; CARB 24.3g; FIBER 3g; CHOL 234mg; IRON 2.5mg; SODIUM 671mg; CALC 239mg

nutrition note

Solutions to Breakfast Barriers

Whether you're running late for the bus or everyone woke up on the wrong side of the bed, getting your family to eat breakfast on busy mornings can be hard. Here are some quick solutions to navigate around the most common breakfast barriers from kids.

IF your child says he's not hungry, **THEN** offer milk or a smoothie. Some nutrients are better than none at all, and while you may not be able to get him to eat anything, kids will often drink something. Milk is a good option because it has both carbs and protein. However, it may not provide enough energy to get him through the morning, so try a smoothie to give him a healthy dose of energy and nutrients.

IF your child doesn't have time to sit down and eat, **THEN** have meal options that can be eaten in the car or on the bus. Dry whole-grain cereal, yogurt, fresh fruit, and cheese sticks are just a few portable ideas that can be mixed and matched to provide a well-balanced meal en route.

IF your child doesn't want any of the breakfast options you've offered, **THEN** think outside the cereal box. Just because a food isn't usually considered a breakfast item doesn't mean it's not healthy in the morning. A small peanut butter or turkey sandwich on whole-grain bread paired with fresh fruit and milk can fuel both kids and adults.

Strawberry Yogurt Scones

Scones are similar to biscuits but slightly sweeter. Look for dried strawberries on the grocery aisle near raisins and other dried fruits. You can use fresh strawberries in place of the dried, if you like. Just substitute ¾ cup chopped fresh strawberries for the dried, and omit the milk.

Young Chefs can:

- Help pat dough into a circle
- Measure strawberries and add to dough
- Sprinkle dough with sugar

Older Chefs can:

- Help cut butter into small pieces with dinner knife
- Knead dough

6.75 ounces all-purpose flour (about 1½ cups)
3.2 ounces whole-wheat flour (about ⅔ cup)
½   cup sugar
2   teaspoons baking powder
½   teaspoon baking soda
¼   teaspoon salt
3   tablespoons chilled butter, cut into small pieces
¾   cup dried strawberries, chopped
1   large egg white
¼   cup 1% low-fat milk
½   teaspoon grated orange rind
1   (6-ounce) carton strawberry fat-free yogurt
Cooking spray
2   teaspoons sugar

1. Preheat oven to 400°. **2. Weigh** or lightly spoon flours into dry measuring cups; level with a knife. Combine flours, ½ cup sugar, and next 3 ingredients in a medium bowl, stirring with a whisk. Cut in butter with a pastry blender or 2 knives until mixture resembles coarse meal. Stir in dried strawberries.

Place egg white in a medium bowl; stir with a whisk. Stir in milk, rind, and yogurt. Add strawberry yogurt mixture to flour mixture, stirring just until moist. **3. Turn** dough out onto a lightly floured surface; knead lightly 4 times with floured hands. Pat into a 7½-inch circle on a baking sheet coated with cooking spray. Cut into 12 wedges, cutting into but not through dough; sprinkle with 2 teaspoons sugar. **4. Bake** at 400° for 20 minutes or until lightly browned. Let cool on pan 5 minutes before serving. **Yield:** 12 servings (serving size: 1 scone).

CALORIES 173; FAT 3.3g (sat 1.9g, mono 0.8g, poly 0.2g); PROTEIN 3.9g; CARB 32.2g; FIBER 1.6g; CHOL 8mg; IRON 1.1mg; SODIUM 205mg; CALC 75mg

Baby Buttermilk Biscuits

These tender, old-fashioned biscuits are much lower in fat and sodium than fast-food biscuits and are just as tasty.

Young Chefs can:

- Help cut dough with biscuit cutter
- Place biscuits on baking sheet

Older Chefs can:

- Help cut butter into small pieces with dinner knife
- Knead dough and measure dimensions with a ruler

9   ounces all-purpose flour (about 2 cups)
2½   teaspoons baking powder
½   teaspoon salt
5   tablespoons chilled butter, cut into small pieces
¾   cup nonfat buttermilk
3   tablespoons honey

1. Preheat oven to 400°. **2. Weigh** or lightly spoon flour into dry measuring cups; level with a knife.

Combine flour, baking powder, and salt in a large bowl; cut in butter with a pastry blender or 2 knives until mixture resembles coarse meal. Chill 10 minutes. **3. Combine** buttermilk and honey, stirring with a whisk. Add buttermilk mixture to flour mixture, stirring just until moist. **4. Turn** dough out onto a lightly floured surface; knead lightly 4 times. Roll dough into a ($\frac{1}{2}$-inch-thick) 9 x 5-inch rectangle; dust top of dough with flour. Fold dough crosswise into thirds (as if folding a piece of paper to fit into an envelope). Re-roll dough into a ($\frac{1}{2}$-inch-thick) 9 x 5-inch rectangle; dust top of dough with flour. Fold dough crosswise into thirds; gently roll or pat to $\frac{3}{4}$-inch thickness. Cut dough with a $1\frac{3}{4}$-inch biscuit cutter to form 18 dough rounds. Place dough rounds, 1 inch apart, on a baking sheet lined with parchment paper. **5. Bake** at 400° for 12 minutes or until golden. Remove from pan; cool 2 minutes on wire racks. Serve warm. **Yield:** 18 servings (serving size: 1 biscuit).

CALORIES 94; FAT 3.3g (sat 2.1g, mono 0.8g, poly 0.2g); PROTEIN 1.9g; CARB 14.3g; FIBER 0.4g; CHOL 9mg; IRON 0.7mg; SODIUM 153mg; CALC 49mg

Pumpkin Biscuit variation: Add $1\frac{1}{4}$ teaspoons pumpkin pie spice to flour mixture. Decrease buttermilk to $\frac{1}{3}$ cup; whisk $\frac{3}{4}$ cup canned pumpkin into buttermilk mixture. Bake at 400° for 12 to 13 minutes. **Yield:** 18 servings (serving size: 1 biscuit).

CALORIES 96; FAT 3.3g (sat 2.1g, mono 0.8g, poly 0.1g); PROTEIN 1.9g; CARB 14.9g; FIBER 0.7g; CHOL 8mg; IRON 0.8mg; SODIUM 148mg; CALC 45mg

"I liked the biscuits because they were bite-sized. I'd want to eat them with apple butter."

Ashley, age 12

Sweet Potato and Pecan Flapjacks

Sweet potato gives these pancakes a healthy dose of beta carotene, an antioxidant that also keeps eyes healthy. For convenience, roast a sweet potato the night before, or use canned mashed sweet potato. Drizzle with maple syrup and butter, and serve with a side of fresh fruit.

Young Chefs can:

- Measure pecans
- Help add dry measured ingredients to mixing bowl

Older Chefs can:

- Combine milk and wet ingredients
- Whisk milk mixture
- Measure sweet potato

5.6 ounces all-purpose flour (about 1¼ cups)
¼ cup chopped pecans, toasted
3 tablespoons yellow cornmeal
2 teaspoons baking powder
½ teaspoon salt
½ teaspoon ground cinnamon
1 cup fat-free milk
1 cup mashed cooked sweet potato
3 tablespoons brown sugar
1 tablespoon canola oil
½ teaspoon vanilla extract
2 large egg yolks
2 large egg whites, lightly beaten
Cooking spray

1. **Weigh** or lightly spoon flour into dry measuring cups; level with a knife. Combine flour and next 5 ingredients in a large bowl, stirring with a whisk.
2. **Combine** milk and next 5 ingredients, stirring with a whisk until smooth; add to flour mixture, stirring just until combined. Beat egg whites with a mixer at high speed until soft peaks form; fold egg whites into batter. Let batter stand 10 minutes. **3. Heat** a nonstick griddle or nonstick skillet over medium-high heat. Coat pan with cooking spray. Spoon about ¼ cup batter per pancake onto pan. Cook 2 minutes or until tops are covered with bubbles and edges look cooked. Carefully turn pancakes over; cook 2 minutes or until bottoms are lightly browned. **Yield:** 8 servings (serving size: 2 pancakes).

CALORIES 199; FAT 5.7g (sat 0.8g, mono 3g, poly 1.5g); PROTEIN 5.8g; CARB 31.2g; FIBER 2.1g; CHOL 53mg; IRON 1.6mg; SODIUM 286mg; CALC 125mg

Banana-Cinnamon Waffles

Young Chefs can:

- Peel banana
- Help add dry measured ingredients to mixing bowl

Older Chefs can:

- Mash banana
- Crack eggs

4.5 ounces all-purpose flour (about 1 cup)
2.4 ounces whole-wheat flour (about ¹/₂ cup)
1.3 ounces buckwheat flour (about ¹/₄ cup)
¹/₄ cup ground flaxseed
2 tablespoons sugar
1¹/₂ teaspoons baking powder
¹/₂ teaspoon ground cinnamon
¹/₄ teaspoon salt
1¹/₂ cups fat-free milk
3 tablespoons butter, melted
2 large eggs, lightly beaten
³/₄ cup mashed ripe banana (1 large)
Cooking spray

1. Weigh or lightly spoon flours into dry measuring cups; level with a knife. Combine flours, flaxseed, and next 4 ingredients in a medium bowl, stirring with a whisk. **2. Combine** milk, butter, and eggs, stirring with a whisk; add milk mixture to flour mixture, stirring until blended. Fold in mashed banana. **3. Preheat** waffle iron. Coat waffle iron with cooking spray. **4. Spoon** about ¹/₄ cup batter per 4-inch waffle onto hot waffle iron, spreading batter evenly to edges. Cook 3 to 4 minutes or until steaming stops; repeat procedure with remaining batter. **Yield:** 8 servings (serving size: 2 waffles).

CALORIES 220; FAT 7.7g (sat 3.4g, mono 1.9g, poly 1.5g); PROTEIN 7.3g; CARB 31.7g; FIBER 3.6g; CHOL 65mg; IRON 1.7mg; SODIUM 217mg; CALC 127mg

Waffles with Fruit and Yogurt

Fresh fruit and yogurt transform ordinary frozen waffles into a special breakfast that's quick to prepare. For fun, your kids can create funny faces on the waffles with the yogurt and fruit toppings.

Young Chefs can:

- Measure blueberries and raspberries
- Sprinkle wheat germ

Older Chefs can:

- Stir honey into yogurt
- Top waffles with yogurt and fruit

1 cup sliced strawberries
1 cup blueberries
1 cup raspberries
1 tablespoon sugar
2 cups creamy vanilla low-fat yogurt
2 tablespoons honey
4 whole-grain frozen waffles
2 teaspoons toasted wheat germ

1. Combine first 4 ingredients; let stand 20 minutes or overnight. **2. Spoon** yogurt into a bowl; stir in honey. **3. Toast** waffles according to package directions. Place 1 waffle on each of 4 plates. Top waffles evenly with fruit, yogurt mixture, and wheat germ. Serve immediately. **Yield:** 4 servings (serving size: 1 waffle, ³/₄ cup fruit, ¹/₂ cup yogurt mixture, and ¹/₂ teaspoon wheat germ).

CALORIES 302; FAT 5.1g (sat 1g, mono 0.1g, poly 0.3g); PROTEIN 6.1g; CARB 62.1g; FIBER 6.9g; CHOL 7mg; IRON 1.4mg; SODIUM 215mg; CALC 161mg

Yeast—Watch It Grow

Ever wonder how sticky dough transforms into light fluffy rolls or loaves of bread? It's usually thanks to a tiny organism called yeast. When yeast grows, it converts sugar or starch in the dough into a gas called carbon dioxide. The carbon dioxide gas is what helps the dough to rise or leaven as it cooks.

Just like a person, yeast needs a few things to survive—food, water, and a warm environment. In Whole-Wheat Cinnamon Rolls, the yeast is added to warm water and milk and then allowed to sit for a few minutes. The natural sugar in milk provides food for the yeast, and the warm liquid helps the yeast grow. Watch closely and you'll see the yeast bubble and expand. After 5 minutes, the yeast has grown enough to leaven the rolls when they bake, and the remaining ingredients can be added.

Kneading the dough helps mix the yeast fully into the flour's starch and protein. Mixing the yeast in by kneading allows the rolls to fully rise to their potential when the carbon dioxide is made during baking. Since kneading takes a little time, there is dough you can buy that already has yeast mixed into it and doesn't require kneading, like the refrigerated pizza crust dough used in Sausage, Egg, and Cheese Breakfast Braid on page 42.

Whole-Wheat Cinnamon Rolls

Brown sugar and cinnamon make a gooey sweet filling while powdered sugar dissolves into a creamy glaze that's drizzled over the top of these breakfast treats.

Young Chefs can:

- Sprinkle raisins over dough
- Help roll up dough

Older Chefs can:

- Help knead dough
- Combine brown sugar and spices, and sprinkle over dough
- Help drizzle glaze

DOUGH:

1½ packages dry yeast (about 3¼ teaspoons)
¾   cup warm fat-free milk (100° to 110°)
¼   cup warm water (100° to 110°)
¼   cup butter, softened
¼   cup honey
½   teaspoon salt
1½ teaspoons fresh lemon juice
1   large egg
1   large egg white
11.25 ounces all-purpose flour (about 2½ cups), divided
7.2 ounces whole-wheat flour (about 1½ cups)
Cooking spray

FILLING:

¼   cup packed brown sugar
1½ tablespoons ground cinnamon
⅛   teaspoon ground nutmeg
⅓   cup raisins

GLAZE:

1¼ cups powdered sugar, sifted
1   teaspoon vanilla extract
5   teaspoons fat-free milk

1. **To prepare dough,** combine yeast, warm milk, and ¼ cup warm water in a large bowl; let stand 5 minutes or until foamy. Stir butter and next 5 ingredients into yeast mixture. Weigh or lightly spoon flours into dry measuring cups; level with a knife. Add 9 ounces (about 2 cups) all-purpose flour and whole-wheat flour to yeast mixture, stirring until a soft dough forms. Turn dough out onto a floured surface. Knead 5 minutes or until smooth and elastic, adding remaining ½ cup all-purpose flour, 1 tablespoon at a time, to prevent dough from sticking to hands (dough will feel sticky). Place dough in a large bowl coated with cooking spray, turning to coat top. Cover and let rise in a warm place (85°), free from drafts, 1 hour or until doubled in size. (Gently press two fingers into dough. If indentation remains, dough has risen enough.) Punch down dough; roll into a 16 x 12–inch rectangle on a floured surface. Coat surface of dough with cooking spray. **2. To prepare filling,** combine brown sugar, cinnamon, and nutmeg; sprinkle over dough, leaving a ½-inch border. Sprinkle raisins over dough, pressing gently into dough. Tightly roll up rectangle, starting with a long edge, pressing firmly to eliminate air pockets; pinch seam to seal. Cut dough into 16 rolls. Place rolls, cut sides up, in a 13 x 9–inch metal baking pan coated with cooking spray. Cover and let rise 45 minutes or until doubled in size. **3. Preheat** oven to 375°. **4. Uncover** rolls. Bake at 375° for 19 minutes or until lightly browned. Cool in pan on a wire rack. **5. To prepare glaze,** place powdered sugar and vanilla in a small bowl. Add 5 teaspoons milk, 1 teaspoon at a time, stirring to form a thick glaze. Drizzle glaze evenly over rolls. **Yield:** 16 servings (serving size: 1 roll).

CALORIES 231; FAT 3.8g (sat 2g, mono 0.9g, poly 0.3g); PROTEIN 5.3g; CARB 45.5g; FIBER 2.8g; CHOL 21mg; IRON 1.8mg; SODIUM 110mg; CALC 39mg

Quick Breakfast Burritos

Young Chefs can:

- Sprinkle cheese on eggs
- Roll up burritos

Older Chefs can:

- Crack eggs
- Combine and whisk first five ingredients

¼ teaspoon chopped fresh oregano
⅛ teaspoon salt
⅛ teaspoon black pepper
3 eggs, lightly beaten
3 egg whites, lightly beaten
4 (7½-inch) 96% fat-free whole-wheat flour tortillas
Cooking spray
¼ cup finely chopped onion
1 cup (4 ounces) preshredded reduced-fat 4-cheese Mexican blend cheese
1 cup fresh salsa

1. **Combine** first 5 ingredients in a bowl, stirring with a whisk. Heat tortillas according to package directions; keep warm. **2. Heat** a large nonstick skillet over medium heat. Coat pan with cooking spray. Add egg mixture and onion to pan. Cook, without stirring, 2 minutes or until mixture sets on bottom. Draw a spatula across bottom of pan to form curds. (Do not stir constantly.) Cook 2 minutes or until egg mixture is thickened, but still moist. Remove from heat. **3. Divide** egg mixture evenly among warm tortillas. Top with ¼ cup cheese and ¼ cup salsa. Fold opposite sides of tortillas over filling; roll up. Serve immediately. **Yield:** 4 servings (serving size: 1 burrito).

CALORIES 298; FAT 12.2g (sat 4.2g, mono 1.4g, poly 0.5g); PROTEIN 20.2g; CARB 31g; FIBER 4g; CHOL 179mg; IRON 2.4mg; SODIUM 712mg; CALC 437mg

Easy French Toast Casserole

French bread with a soft crust works best here because it is easier to cut. Garnish with fresh strawberry slices, and serve with a glass of fat-free or 1% low-fat milk.

Young Chefs can:

- Help measure brown sugar
- Place bread slices in egg mixture

Older Chefs can:

- Crack and whisk eggs
- Pour leftover egg mixture over bread slices

$2/3$ cup packed dark brown sugar
2 tablespoons butter
2 tablespoons dark corn syrup
Cooking spray
2 large eggs
1 large egg white
$1\frac{1}{2}$ cups 1% low-fat milk
1 teaspoon vanilla extract
$1/4$ teaspoon salt
6 (1-inch-thick) French bread slices
2 tablespoons finely chopped toasted pecans
Strawberry slices (optional)

1. Combine first 3 ingredients in a small, heavy saucepan. Cook over medium heat until bubbly and sugar dissolves, stirring constantly. Pour sugar mixture into an 11 x 7–inch glass or ceramic baking dish coated with cooking spray, spreading evenly over bottom of dish. **2. Combine** eggs and egg white in a large bowl, stirring with a whisk until blended. Stir in milk, vanilla, and salt. Dip bread slices in egg mixture, and arrange over sugar mixture. Pour any remaining egg mixture evenly over bread slices. Cover and refrigerate overnight. **3. Preheat** oven to 350°. **4. Bake,** uncovered, at 350° for 30 minutes or until lightly browned. **5. Place** 1 toast piece on each of 6 plates. Sprinkle each serving with 1 teaspoon pecans. Garnish with strawberry slices, if desired. **Yield:** 6 servings.

CALORIES 279; FAT 8.3g (sat 3.6g, mono 2.8g, poly 1.1g); PROTEIN 7.5g; CARB 44.9g; FIBER 0.7g; CHOL 84mg; IRON 1.4mg; SODIUM 339mg; CALC 116mg

> "It was really tasty, and I don't usually like casseroles.
> I'd eat this with biscuits or toast and cheese grits."
>
> Jarret, age 9

Breakfast Sausage Casserole

Assemble and refrigerate the casserole the night before, and just pop it in the oven the next morning.

Young Chefs can:

- Tear bread into cubes
- Measure bread cubes in measuring cups

Older Chefs can:

- Measure cheese
- Combine sausage, bread, and cheese

Cooking spray

1   (16-ounce) package frozen turkey breakfast
    sausage, thawed
8   (1½-ounce) sourdough bread slices,
    cut into 1-inch cubes (about 8 cups)
¾   cup (3 ounces) shredded sharp cheddar cheese,
    divided
2½ cups 1% low-fat milk
8   large egg whites
1   tablespoon Dijon mustard

1. Heat a large nonstick skillet over medium-high heat. Coat pan with cooking spray. Add sausage to pan; cook 5 minutes or until browned, stirring to crumble. Drain. **2. Combine** sausage, bread, and ½ cup cheese in a large bowl. Combine milk, egg whites, and mustard in a separate bowl, stirring with a whisk. Pour milk mixture over bread mixture, tossing until bread is moistened. Arrange bread in a 13 x 9-inch glass or ceramic baking dish coated with cooking spray. Cover and refrigerate 8 hours or overnight. Uncover and sprinkle with remaining ¼ cup cheese. **3. Preheat** oven to 350°. **4. Bake,** uncovered, at 350° for 1 hour and 5 minutes or until set and lightly browned. Let stand 15 minutes before serving. **Yield:** 8 servings (serving size: ⅛ of casserole).

CALORIES 286; FAT 10.2g (sat 4.8g, mono 1.8g, poly 1g); PROTEIN 22.1g; CARB 26.6g; FIBER 1.3g; CHOL 58mg; IRON 2.7mg; SODIUM 792mg; CALC 224mg

kitchen classroom
A Good Start

Sourdough bread, known for its slightly sour—but tasty—flavor, provides the right amount of tang to this cheesy egg dish. The acidic flavor is due to good bacteria in the dough that help the bread to rise. This is a different leavening method than yeast breads use (see page 38) and requires a "starter" or a small piece of dough that contains yeast and bacteria. The starter must be allowed to grow by feeding it flour and letting it sit at room temperature. The bacteria in the starter grow more rapidly than the yeast; after a few days the starter can be incorporated into a dough and baked. Gases from the bacteria help to leaven the bread loaf and give it an acidic flavor. Because of its acidity, sourdough breads are more resistant to spoiling than yeast breads.

Sausage, Egg, and Cheese Breakfast Braid

Save this filling breakfast bread for a morning when you aren't rushed. Young bakers will enjoy helping fill and then braid the dough. Feel free to substitute a milder cheese in place of the Monterey Jack.

Young Chefs can:

- Unroll dough
- Sprinkle cheese

Older Chefs can:

- Pat dough into rectangle and measure dimensions
- Brush dough with egg white

1	(13.8-ounce) can refrigerated pizza crust dough

Cooking spray

1	tablespoon olive oil
¼	cup chopped onion
4	ounces chicken sausage with apples, chopped
2	large eggs, lightly beaten
½	cup (2 ounces) shredded Monterey Jack cheese
¼	cup (1 ounce) shredded mild cheddar cheese
1	large egg white, lightly beaten

1. Preheat oven to 425°. **2. Unroll** dough onto a baking sheet coated with cooking spray; pat into a 15 x 10-inch rectangle. **3. Heat** oil in a large skillet over medium heat. Add onion and sausage; cook 8 minutes or until lightly browned. Stir in eggs; cook 1 minute or until set. Remove from heat. **4. Sprinkle** Monterey Jack cheese lengthwise down center of dough, leaving a 2½-inch border on each side. Spoon egg mixture over cheese. Sprinkle cheddar cheese over egg mixture. **5. Make** 2-inch-long diagonal cuts about 1 inch apart on both sides of dough to within ½ inch of filling using a sharp knife or kitchen shears. Alternately arrange strips diagonally over filling. Fold ends under to seal. Brush with egg white. **6. Bake** at 425° for 15 minutes or until golden brown. Let stand 5 minutes. Cut into slices. **Yield:** 6 servings (serving size: 1 slice).

CALORIES 294; FAT 12.4g (sat 4.7g, mono 3.1g, poly 0.6g); PROTEIN 13.4g; CARB 33g; FIBER 0.6g; CHOL 98mg; IRON 2.4mg; SODIUM 679mg; CALC 115mg

Bacon and Egg Breakfast Pizza

Bacon, cheese, and potatoes make for tasty toppings on this kid-approved pizza. Reheat leftovers on a griddle or in a skillet over medium heat to get a crisp crust without overcooking the filling.

Young Chefs can:

- Unroll dough
- Help top dough with toppings

Older Chefs can:

- Press dough triangles together
- Pour egg whites over cheese
- Sprinkle salt, pepper, and cheese

1   (8-ounce) can reduced-fat refrigerated crescent dinner roll dough

Cooking spray

1   cup frozen shredded or diced hash brown potatoes, thawed

6   center-cut bacon slices, cooked and crumbled

1   cup (4 ounces) reduced-fat shredded extrasharp cheddar cheese

8   large egg whites, lightly beaten

¼   teaspoon salt

⅛   teaspoon freshly ground black pepper

2   tablespoons grated fresh Parmesan cheese

1. Preheat oven to 375°. **2. Unroll** dough, and separate into triangles. Press triangles together to form a single 10-inch round crust on a 12-inch pizza pan coated with cooking spray. Crimp edges of dough with fingers to form a rim. **3. Top** prepared dough with potatoes, bacon, and cheddar cheese. Carefully pour egg whites over cheese; sprinkle with salt, pepper, and Parmesan cheese. **4. Bake** at 375° for 23 minutes or until crust is browned. Cut into wedges. **Yield:** 8 servings (serving size: 1 wedge).

CALORIES 192; FAT 10.1g (sat 4.9g, mono 1.9g, poly 1.0g); PROTEIN 11.6g; CARB 14.5g; FIBER 0.1g; CHOL 15mg; IRON 1.4mg; SODIUM 560mg; CALC 132mg

Lunch

Packing in nutrients at school and home

Lunch

The lunch meal is a challenge for many. Parents with children at home strive to think of fresh new meal ideas outside of the classic peanut butter and jelly. Parents with children in school must try to pack tasty, healthy meals each morning or hope that their children spend their lunchroom money wisely. No matter the setting, involving your children in the meal planning and preparation increases the likelihood that they will eat lunch and enjoy it.

Turkey-Apple Grilled Cheese Sandwiches

Cheddar cheese and honey mustard complement tart apple and smoked turkey for a tasty spin on the every-day turkey sandwich. Cut the leftover Granny Smith apple into slices to serve with the sandwiches.

Young Chefs can:

- Count out slices of bread, apple, and cheese
- Top bread with turkey, apple, and cheese

Older Chefs can:

- Spread dressing over bread slices
- Coat sandwiches with cooking spray

2   tablespoons honey mustard dressing
4   (1-ounce) 100% whole-wheat small-slice bread
     slices
3   ounces lean deli smoked turkey breast
6   thin slices Granny Smith apple
2   (1-ounce) slices reduced-fat mild cheddar cheese
Butter-flavored cooking spray

1. Spread dressing evenly over bread slices. Top 2 bread slices evenly with turkey, apple slices, cheese, and remaining 2 bread slices. **2. Heat** a large non-stick skillet over medium heat. Coat pan with cooking spray. Add sandwiches to pan; cook 3 minutes or until lightly browned. Coat tops of sandwiches with cooking spray. Turn sandwiches over; cook 3 minutes or until cheese melts. **Yield:** 2 servings (serving size: 1 sandwich).

CALORIES 298; FAT 6.2g (sat 1.4g, mono 0.6g, poly 0.1g); PROTEIN 24.3g; CARB 34.4g; FIBER 5.1g; CHOL 25mg; IRON 2.3mg; SODIUM 775mg; CALC 171mg

kitchen classroom
Cheddar Cheese Lingo

Perplexed as to what the words mild, medium, sharp, or extra sharp mean on cheddar cheese packages? These terms refer to the cheese's sharpness or amount of tang. Typically, the longer a cheese is aged, the tangier the flavor. For sensitive or picky palates, the best bet is to opt for mild or medium cheddar. For more adventuresome eaters, sharp or extrasharp adds a nice kick of flavor, especially to potatoes and pastas.

"I like this because it has so much flavor. I would definitely eat a whole one."

Nathan, age 6

Grilled Turkey and Ham Sandwiches

Turkey and honey mustard dress up the basic ham and cheese melt. This sandwich is also good cold if you're in a hurry or want to pack it to go.

Young Chefs can:

• Stir together mayonnaise and mustard
• Count out slices of bread, turkey, ham, tomato, and cheese

Older Chefs can:

• Spread mayonnaise mixture on bread
• Assemble sandwiches
• Coat sandwiches with cooking spray

1	tablespoon light mayonnaise
1	tablespoon honey mustard
8	(1-ounce) 100% whole-wheat small-slice bread slices
4	(1-ounce) deli, lower-sodium turkey slices
4	(1-ounce) deli, lower-sodium baked ham slices
4	(½-ounce) reduced-fat mild cheddar cheese slices
8	(¼-inch-thick) tomato slices

Cooking spray

1. Combine mayonnaise and mustard in a small bowl. Spread about 1 teaspoon mayonnaise mixture over 1 side of each bread slice. Top each of 4 bread slices with 1 turkey slice, 1 ham slice, 1 cheese slice, and 2 tomato slices. Top with remaining bread slices.

2. Heat a large nonstick skillet over medium-high heat. Coat pan with cooking spray. Add sandwiches to pan; cook 3 minutes or until lightly browned. Coat tops of sandwiches with cooking spray. Turn sandwiches over; cook 2 minutes or until cheese melts.

Yield: 4 servings (serving size: 1 sandwich).

CALORIES 305; FAT 8.4g (sat 2.5g, mono 0g, poly 0.1g); PROTEIN 22g; CARB 29.2g; FIBER 5.1g; CHOL 34mg; IRON 2.2mg; SODIUM 788mg; CALC 153mg

meals made easy =

Grilled Turkey and Ham Sandwiches + baby carrots +

Toasted Ham and Cheese Bagel Sandwiches

Thin bagels are perfect for smaller appetites and are easier to eat as part of a sandwich. Make a complete lunch or breakfast meal by pairing this sandwich with baby carrots or orange sections and a cup of low-fat milk to meet over half of most kids' daily calcium needs.

Young Chefs can:

- Pull four lettuce leaves off head of lettuce
- Layer ham, and sprinkle cheese

Older Chefs can:

- Spread cream cheese mixture on bagels
- Top sandwich with lettuce and bagel top

¼	cup (2 ounces) tub-style light cream cheese
1	tablespoon chopped fresh basil
1	teaspoon Dijon mustard
4	whole-wheat thin bagels, lightly toasted
4	ounces low-fat deli ham
½	cup (2 ounces) reduced-fat shredded sharp cheddar cheese
4	green leaf lettuce leaves

1. Preheat broiler. **2. Combine** first 3 ingredients in a small bowl. **3. Spread** about 1 tablespoon cream cheese mixture over cut sides of each bagel. Layer 1 ounce ham and 2 tablespoons cheddar cheese over cream cheese on bagel bottoms. Place on a baking sheet. Broil 2 minutes or until cheese melts. Remove from oven, and top with lettuce leaves; cover with bagel tops. Serve immediately. **Yield:** 4 servings (serving size: 1 sandwich).

CALORIES 208; FAT 6.3g (sat 3.6g, mono 0g, poly 0g); PROTEIN 15.3g; CARB 23.3g; FIBER 6.3g; CHOL 24mg; IRON 1.1mg; SODIUM 589mg; CALC 220mg

Ranch Chicken Pita Pockets

You can adapt these easy sandwiches to suit any taste. Try substituting wraps in place of pitas or smoked turkey instead of chicken. Or use a blue cheese dressing for a tangy kick.

Young Chefs can:

- Help shred lettuce
- Add ingredients to bowl

Older Chefs can:

- Help shred chicken
- Help spoon mixture into pita halves

2	cups shredded romaine lettuce
1½	cups shredded skinless, boneless rotisserie chicken breast
1	cup chopped tomato (about 2 medium)
4	center-cut bacon slices, cooked and crumbled
⅓	cup light ranch dressing
4	whole-wheat pitas, warmed and halved

1. Combine first 4 ingredients in a bowl. Add dressing; toss well. Spoon lettuce mixture evenly into pita halves.
Yield: 4 servings (serving size: 2 pita halves).

CALORIES 337; FAT 9.7g (sat 1.6g, mono 1g, poly 1g); PROTEIN 25.7g; CARB 39.8g; FIBER 5.9g; CHOL 62mg; IRON 2.6mg; SODIUM 326mg; CALC 35mg

nutrition note
Pack a Safe Lunchbox

Food safety is a priority when packing meals to go. The key is keeping foods out of the temperature danger zone (40° to 140°F), the range where bacteria grow best. This is easy when packed lunches are refrigerated, but most school kids don't have access to refrigerators—lunches are stored in lockers or backpacks. Here are tips to help keep both food and kids safe.

Help cold food stay cold. Invest in an insulated lunch bag to help refrigerated foods like lunch meat, cheese, yogurt, and milk stay cold. A small ice pack, frozen juice box, or refrigerated yogurt that's been frozen can also help, as well as provide an icy cold drink or side dish.

Prep the night before. Make sandwiches and salads the night before, and then store in the refrigerator overnight. This gives prepared food time to chill to 40° or below.

Help hot food stay hot. Use an insulated airtight container to pack soup. Before packing, place hot water in the thermos container for a few minutes, pour it out, and then add the soup and secure the lid tightly.

Pack just enough. Only pack what you think your child will eat. This prevents uneaten food being wasted since leftovers should be discarded.

Consider safer foods. Some foods, such as canned tuna, peanut butter, jelly, whole fruits, vegetables, nuts, crackers, chips, and pickles, are safe stored at room temperature. Substitute these for some of the more temperature-sensitive foods such as lunch meats and dairy products.

lunch

Southwestern Roast Beef Wraps

Refried beans help hold ingredients in place. For a variation, thinly sliced turkey also works well in these portable sandwiches.

Young Chefs can:

- Top tortillas with roast beef
- Measure and sprinkle cheese

Older Chefs can:

- Stir together first eight ingredients
- Spread beans over wraps
- Spoon corn mixture in tortillas

2	tablespoons minced red onion
2	tablespoons fresh lime juice
1	tablespoon extra-virgin olive oil
½	teaspoon ground cumin
⅛	teaspoon salt
⅛	teaspoon freshly ground black pepper
1	cup frozen whole-kernel corn, thawed
½	cup chopped fresh cilantro
1	(16-ounce) can reduced-fat refried beans
1	(11.2-ounce) package light stone-ground whole-wheat wraps
9	ounces lean deli roast beef
¾	cup (3 ounces) shredded Monterey Jack cheese

1. Combine first 6 ingredients in a bowl, stirring with a spoon. Add corn and cilantro; toss until coated.

2. Spread refried beans on 1 side of each wrap. Top wraps evenly with beef. Spoon corn mixture evenly over beef, and sprinkle evenly with cheese. Roll up wraps, and wrap in foil or wax paper. Refrigerate until thoroughly chilled. **Yield:** 6 servings (serving size: 1 wrap).

CALORIES 364; FAT 11g (sat 3.5g, mono 3g, poly 0.5g); PROTEIN 23.6g; CARB 41.9g; FIBER 6.9g; CHOL 36mg; IRON 3.6mg; SODIUM 680mg; CALC 123mg

"I like it being in a wrap. I would eat it with chips and yogurt."

Anna, age 6

Curried Tuna Wraps

Whole-wheat wraps deliver a nutty taste as well as extra fiber and B vitamins. If you want an extra punch of flavor, serve with a side of mango chutney for dipping.

Young Chefs can:

- Tear lettuce leaves
- Pour tuna in colander or strainer to drain

Older Chefs can:

- Stir together measured ingredients
- Help spoon tuna on tortillas and assemble wraps

¼   cup light mayonnaise
1   tablespoon hoisin sauce
1   teaspoon curry powder
¼   teaspoon salt
1   (12-ounce) can solid white tuna in water, drained and flaked
2   tablespoons minced red onion
2   tablespoons raisins
4   (8-inch) whole-wheat flour tortillas
2   cups torn green leaf lettuce

1. Combine first 4 ingredients in a large bowl, stirring with a spoon. Stir in tuna, onion, and raisins, breaking up any large chunks of tuna with a spoon. **2. Spoon** about ⅓ cup tuna mixture down center of each tortilla.

Top each with ½ cup lettuce; roll up. Wrap in plastic wrap or foil, and chill until serving. **Yield:** 4 servings (serving size: 1 wrap).

CALORIES 212; FAT 9.9g (sat 0.8g, mono 0.1g, poly 0.1g); PROTEIN 18.8g; CARB 15g; FIBER 3.8g; CHOL 30mg; IRON 1.5mg; SODIUM 341mg; CALC 76mg

meals made easy

Curried Tuna Wraps

baked sweet potato chips

fat-free or 1 % low-fat milk

Warm Tortellini and Vegetable Salad

Despite its green color, pesto is a food many kids like when it's mixed with pasta. Pasta salads tossed with pesto also keep well in lunch bags. For younger kids, try substituting a whole-grain rotini or macaroni that's easier to eat.

Young Chefs can:

- Measure thinly sliced zucchini
- Sprinkle cheese

Older Chefs can:

- Help sauté zucchini with adult supervision
- Pour pesto mixture over pasta mixture

1   (9-ounce) package fresh three-cheese tortellini
Cooking spray
1   teaspoon bottled minced garlic
2   small zucchini, halved lengthwise and thinly sliced
      (about 2 cups)
1   cup chopped plum tomato
1½ tablespoons commercial pesto
⅛   teaspoon salt
2   tablespoons preshredded fresh Parmesan cheese

1. Cook pasta according to package directions, omitting salt and fat. Drain in a colander over a bowl, reserving 2 tablespoons cooking liquid. **2. While pasta cooks,** heat a large nonstick skillet over medium-high heat. Heavily coat pan with cooking spray. Add garlic and zucchini; sauté 5 minutes or until zucchini is tender. Remove pan from heat; add pasta and tomato to zucchini mixture, tossing gently. **3. Combine** reserved 2 tablespoons cooking liquid, pesto, and salt in a small bowl. Drizzle over pasta mixture, tossing gently to coat. Sprinkle with cheese. **Yield:** 4 servings (serving size: about 1 cup).

CALORIES 247; FAT 8g (sat 3g, mono 0.2g, poly 0.1g); PROTEIN 11.4g; CARB 33.1g; FIBER 2.7g; CHOL 28mg; IRON 1.5mg; SODIUM 461mg; CALC 145mg

Quick Taco Salad

Fresh salsa makes this Mexican-inspired salad a snap to prepare. You'll find it in refrigerated tubs in the produce section. Baked nacho cheese–flavored chips can add an extra punch of flavor, if desired.

Young Chefs can:

- Measure corn and cheese
- Count out chips

Older Chefs can:

- Help assemble salad on platter
- Sprinkle cheese and green onions

12	ounces ground sirloin
1	cup chopped onion
2	cups fresh salsa
1	cup frozen whole-kernel corn
¼	cup chopped fresh cilantro
50	baked tortilla chips
4	cups shredded romaine lettuce
2	cups chopped plum tomato
1	cup (4 ounces) reduced-fat shredded sharp cheddar cheese
⅓	cup chopped green onions

1. Cook beef and onion in a large nonstick skillet over medium-high heat until browned, stirring to crumble beef. Add salsa and corn; bring to a boil. Stir in cilantro; remove from heat, and keep warm. **2. Layer** chips, lettuce, meat mixture, and tomato on a large platter. Sprinkle with cheese and green onions. Serve immediately. **Yield:** 5 servings (serving size: ⅕ of salad).

CALORIES 358; FAT 14.6g (sat 6.4g, mono 4.1g, poly 1.3g); PROTEIN 22.9g; CARB 28.2g; FIBER 4g; CHOL 61mg; IRON 2.6mg; SODIUM 651mg; CALC 229mg

Simple Tuna Salad

Pair this classic tuna salad with whole-grain crackers or warm pita wedges, or serve as a filling for wraps and pita pockets.

Young Chefs can:

- Pour tuna in colander or strainer to drain
- Measure chopped celery

Older Chefs can:

- Break up big pieces of tuna with a fork
- Combine measured ingredients

1	(12-ounce) can albacore tuna in water, drained and flaked
¾	cup finely chopped celery
½	cup minced sweet onion
⅓	cup light mayonnaise
2	tablespoons chopped bottled roasted red bell peppers
1	tablespoon lemon juice

1. Combine ingredients in a medium bowl. Chill until ready to serve. **Yield:** 4 servings (serving size: ½ cup).

CALORIES 179; FAT 7.8g (sat 1g, mono 0g, poly 0g); PROTEIN 21.4g; CARB 5.7g; FIBER 1.1g; CHOL 43mg; IRON 0.6mg; SODIUM 535mg; CALC 21mg

Couscous Salad with Chicken ⊹ ⊹ fat-free or 1% low-fat milk

Couscous Salad with Chicken

This 20-minute salad is a great way to use leftover chicken. We've added quick-cooking couscous and a light salad dressing for flavor.

Young Chefs can:

• Identify and locate vegetables
• Measure chopped cucumber

Older Chefs can:

• Help cube or shred chicken breast
• Add measured ingredients to cooked couscous

1¼ cups fat-free, lower-sodium chicken broth
1   cup uncooked couscous
1½ cups cubed cooked chicken breast
½   cup thinly sliced green onions (2 large)
½   cup diced tomato
½   cup chopped seeded peeled cucumber
6   tablespoons light olive oil vinaigrette
2   tablespoons crumbled feta cheese

1. Bring broth to a boil in a medium saucepan; gradually stir in couscous. Remove from heat; cover and let stand 5 minutes. **2. Fluff** couscous with a fork; spoon into a large bowl. Let cool slightly. Add chicken and remaining ingredients to couscous; toss gently. **Yield:** 5 servings (serving size: 1 cup).

CALORIES 258; FAT 6.3g (sat 1.3g, mono 0.7g, poly 0.5g); PROTEIN 18.5g; CARB 30.8g; FIBER 2.4g; CHOL 39mg; IRON 1.1mg; SODIUM 363mg; CALC 45mg

Chicken Caesar Salad

Using a precooked rotisserie chicken makes this salad extra easy and fast, although any leftover cooked chicken or grilled fish will work. If sending to school for lunch, pack dressing, croutons, and cheese in containers or zip-top plastic bags separate from the salad.

Young Chefs can:

• Tear lettuce leaves
• Measure croutons

Older Chefs can:

• Help shred chicken breast
• Combine ingredients in bowl

4   cups torn romaine lettuce
¾   cup shredded skinless boneless rotisserie chicken breast (about 3 ounces)
⅓   cup diced red bell pepper
¼   cup light Caesar dressing
⅓   cup fat-free Caesar-flavored croutons
3   tablespoons grated fresh Parmesan cheese

1. Combine first 4 ingredients in a large bowl. Sprinkle with croutons and cheese; toss gently. **Yield:** 2 servings (serving size: 2 cups).

CALORIES 219; FAT 11g (sat 2.7g, mono 1.2g, poly 0.5g); PROTEIN 18.3g; CARB 13.2g; FIBER 2.5g; CHOL 54mg; IRON 1.3mg; SODIUM 695mg; CALC 122mg

Fun with Numbers

Any good chef knows that math skills are essential when cooking. Teaching math while cooking is a great way to make abstract concepts become real for kids, so use time in the kitchen with your child to build these skills. Concepts will vary by age, but there's plenty to be learned by all.

Preschool Age

Counting. Allow children to count out cucumber slices, tortillas, cheese slices, or other ingredients. Counting out items helps reinforce number identification and order.

Beginning addition. Visually demonstrate basic addition with food. For example, one egg plus one egg equals two eggs in the muffin batter.

Size and volume concepts. Measure 1 cup of strawberries, and count the number of strawberries that fit. Then measure 1 cup of blueberries, and do the same. Discuss why the numbers differ and talk about size.

Early Elementary Age

Addition, subtraction, and multiplication. Pose scenarios to challenge your child's math skills such as "How many eggs would we need if we tripled this recipe?" or "How many eggs will we have left in the carton after making these muffins?"

Understanding fractions. Cut sandwiches, cookie bars, or loaves of bread into equal pieces to introduce the concept of fractions. Measuring cups also help children visualize fractions. Have them measure 1 cup of sugar; then have them measure 1 cup of sugar but use ½-cup measuring cups or ¼-cup measuring cups.

Late Elementary Age

Multiplying and dividing fractions. Challenging your child to double, halve, or 1½ times a recipe brings fraction work to a real-life setting as they adjust ingredient measurements.

Volume. Gallons, pints, liters, and ounces are easier to understand when children can see what they look like and pour liquids into measuring cups and pitchers.

Problem solving. Reading and interpreting food labels is a great way to introduce math skills, as well as build nutrition knowledge. After explaining food label basics, ask your child how much protein four servings of milk provide, how many calories are in the entire box of oats, or similar questions using labels on recipe ingredients.

Cashew Chicken Salad

If you have extra cooked chicken on hand, then make this salad, which tosses together in 6 minutes. Mix cashews into the salad, crush and sprinkle them on top, or simply omit them if you'd like. Serve it in a sandwich or simply with whole-grain crackers.

Young Chefs can:

- Measure chopped celery and shredded chicken
- Add celery, chicken, and grapes

Older Chefs can:

- Help slice grapes with dinner knife
- Stir ingredients together

¼ cup vanilla or plain fat-free yogurt

3 tablespoons light mayonnaise

¼ teaspoon curry powder

2 cups shredded cooked
  chicken breast

1 cup sliced red seedless grapes

⅓ cup chopped celery

2 tablespoons chopped salted dry-roasted cashews

1 tablespoon finely chopped green onions

1. Combine first 3 ingredients in a large bowl, stirring with a spoon. Add chicken and remaining ingredients, stirring well to coat. Cover and chill before serving.

Yield: 6 servings (serving size: ½ cup).

CALORIES 146; FAT 5.5g (sat 1.1g, mono 1.4g, poly 0.6g); PROTEIN 15.7g; CARB 8.1g; FIBER 0.5g; CHOL 43mg; IRON 0.8mg; SODIUM 125mg; CALC 33mg

Barley and Beef Soup

Make this soup the night before to allow time for its flavors to develop. Pour hot servings into a thermos to take for lunch, or reheat individual portions in the microwave as needed.

Young Chefs can:

• Identify and locate vegetables
• Measure chopped carrot and celery

Older Chefs can:

• Help measure uncooked barley, water, and tomato puree
• Add barley, broth, and water with adult supervision

Cooking spray
2   cups chopped onion (about 1 large)
1½ cups chopped carrot (about 4 medium)
1   cup chopped celery (about 4 stalks)
1   (17-ounce) refrigerated beef roast au jus
5   garlic cloves, minced
1   cup uncooked pearl barley
5   cups fat-free, lower-sodium beef broth
2   cups water
½   cup tomato puree
½   teaspoon kosher salt
¼   teaspoon freshly ground black pepper
2   bay leaves

meals made easy

Barley and Beef Soup

-+-

-+-

-+-

part-skim mozzarella cheese sticks

1. Heat a large Dutch oven over medium-high heat. Coat pan with cooking spray. Add onion, carrot, and celery to pan; cook 5 minutes, stirring occasionally. **2. While vegetables cook,** heat roast beef according to package directions; drain, discarding drippings. Chop beef into 1-inch pieces. **3. Stir** garlic into vegetables; cook 30 seconds. Stir in beef, barley, and remaining ingredients. Bring to a boil; cover, reduce heat, and simmer 40 minutes or until barley and vegetables are tender, stirring occasionally. Remove and discard bay leaves. **Yield:** 10 servings (serving size: 1 cup).

CALORIES 174; FAT 3.5g (sat 1.5g, mono 0g, poly 0.2g); PROTEIN 13.5g; CARB 23.4g; FIBER 4.6g; CHOL 26mg; IRON 1.5mg; SODIUM 545mg; CALC 29mg

Broccoli and Chicken Noodle Soup

Traditional broccoli cheese soups often have more than 16 grams of fat and 2,000 milligrams of sodium per serving. This soup offers a healthier alternative without sacrificing the delicious flavor. If the broccoli florets are large, break them into smaller pieces at the stalk instead of chopping them; they'll cook more quickly. Thin the soup with milk if needed when reheating.

Young Chefs can:

- Measure sliced mushrooms and broccoli
- Help break vermicelli into pieces

Older Chefs can:

- Add vermicelli to mushroom mixture with adult supervision
- Add chicken and broccoli to cheese mixture with adult supervision

Cooking spray
2   cups chopped onion
1   cup sliced mushrooms
1   garlic clove, minced
3   tablespoons canola oil
1.1   ounces all-purpose flour (about ¼ cup)
4   cups 1% low-fat milk
1   (14.5-ounce) can fat-free, lower-sodium chicken broth
3   ounces uncooked vermicelli, broken into 2-inch pieces
2   cups (8 ounces) shredded light processed cheese
4   cups (1-inch) cubed cooked chicken breast
3   cups small broccoli florets
1   cup half-and-half
1   teaspoon freshly ground black pepper
½   teaspoon salt

1. Heat a Dutch oven over medium-high heat. Coat pan with cooking spray. Add onion, mushrooms, and garlic to pan; sauté 5 minutes or until liquid evaporates, stirring occasionally. **2. Reduce** heat to medium; add canola oil to mushroom mixture, stirring to combine. Sprinkle flour over mushroom mixture; cook, stirring constantly, 2 minutes. Gradually add milk and broth, stirring constantly with a whisk; bring to a boil. Reduce heat to medium-low; cook 5 minutes or until slightly thickened, stirring constantly. **3. Stir** pasta into mushroom mixture; cover and cook 10 minutes. **4. Add** cheese to mushroom mixture, stirring until cheese melts. Add chicken and remaining ingredients to cheese mixture; cover and cook 5 minutes or until broccoli is tender and soup is thoroughly heated.

Yield: 10 servings (serving size: 1 cup).

CALORIES 320; FAT 12.7g (sat 4.9g, mono 4.4g, poly 1.8g); PROTEIN 29.2g; CARB 22.1g; FIBER 1.7g; CHOL 71mg; IRON 1.4mg; SODIUM 696mg; CALC 301mg

Broccoli-Cheese Bakers

Cooking the potatoes in the microwave makes this dish a snap to prepare. If making ahead, top potatoes with cheese but wait to heat just before serving.

Young Chefs can:

- Help combine measured ingredients
- Top stuffed potatoes with cheese

Older Chefs can:

- Pierce potatoes with a fork
- Help scoop out potato pulp
- Help spoon potato mixture into shells

2   medium baking potatoes (about 1¾ pounds)
¾   cup (3 ounces) reduced-fat shredded sharp cheddar cheese, divided
1½   cups broccoli florets, steamed and chopped
⅓   cup reduced-fat sour cream
2   tablespoons yogurt-based spread
½   teaspoon salt
3   center-cut bacon slices, cooked and crumbled

1. Pierce potatoes with a fork; arrange on paper towels in microwave oven. Microwave at HIGH 10 minutes or until done, rearranging potatoes after 5 minutes. Let stand 5 minutes. **2. Cut** each potato in half lengthwise; scoop out pulp, leaving a ¼-inch-thick shell. Combine potato pulp, ¼ cup cheese, and next 5 ingredients. Spoon potato mixture evenly into shells. **3. Top** each potato half with 2 tablespoons cheese. Arrange stuffed potato halves on paper towels in microwave oven. Microwave at HIGH 2 minutes or until thoroughly heated. **Yield:** 4 servings (serving size: 1 potato half).

CALORIES 289; FAT 10.6g (sat 5.1g, mono 0.7g, poly 0.2g); PROTEIN 12.2g; CARB 38.6g; FIBER 3.1g; CHOL 26.7mg; IRON 1.8mg; SODIUM 454mg; CALC 356mg

Brown Rice and Black Bean Burrito

This cheesy burrito got high marks from our Kids Taste-Testing Panel. Plus, it delivers a healthy dose of fiber, calcium, and complex carbs. The rice-and-bean mixture can be prepared ahead, refrigerated, and then reheated when you're ready to assemble burritos.

Young Chefs can:

- Pour beans in colander, and rinse
- Sprinkle cheese
- Help roll up burritos

Older Chefs can:

- Measure chili powder and cumin
- Assemble burritos

½	teaspoon vegetable oil
½	cup chopped onion
1	garlic clove, minced
1	teaspoon chili powder
¼	teaspoon ground cumin
½	(8.8-ounce) package precooked brown rice
¾	cup rinsed and drained black beans
1	(7-ounce) can whole-kernel corn with sweet peppers
¼	cup light sour cream
4	(8-inch) whole-wheat flour tortillas, warmed
½	cup (2 ounces) reduced-fat shredded cheddar cheese
¼	cup fresh salsa

1. Heat oil in a large nonstick skillet over medium-high heat. Add onion and next 3 ingredients; sauté 4 minutes or until onion is tender. Stir in rice, beans, and corn; cook, stirring constantly, 3 minutes or until thoroughly heated. Remove from heat. **2. Spread** 1 tablespoon sour cream on each tortilla; top each with about ½ cup bean mixture, 2 tablespoons cheese, and 1 tablespoon salsa. Fold sides of tortillas over filling, and roll up. **Yield:** 4 servings (serving size: 1 burrito).

CALORIES 260; FAT 9.8g (sat 2.6g, mono 1g, poly 0.5g); PROTEIN 13g; CARB 37.6g; FIBER 7.5g; CHOL 13mg; IRON 1.9mg; SODIUM 751mg; CALC 233mg

meals made easy =

Spinach and Corn Quesadillas + + fat-free chocolate pudding

Spinach and Corn Quesadillas

Cooking the quesadillas together on a baking sheet is much quicker than cooking them separately in a skillet. Adults and more adventuresome young diners can jazz up their quesadillas with jalapeño peppers, chopped green onions, or cilantro.

Young Chefs can:

- Tear spinach leaves
- Measure and sprinkle cheese

Older Chefs can:

- Spray tortillas with cooking spray
- Help spoon spinach mixture onto tortillas

Cooking spray

4   cups torn baby spinach

1   cup frozen whole-kernel corn, thawed and
     drained

4   (8-inch) whole-wheat flour tortillas

1   cup (4 ounces) reduced-fat shredded cheddar
     cheese

½   cup fresh salsa

¼   cup reduced-fat sour cream (optional)

1. Preheat oven to 400°. **2. Heat** a large nonstick skillet over medium-high heat. Coat pan with cooking spray. Add spinach and corn; sauté 1 to 2 minutes or just until spinach wilts. Remove from heat. **3. Coat** 1 side of tortillas with cooking spray. Place tortillas, coated sides down, on a large baking sheet; top evenly with spinach mixture and cheese. Fold tortillas in half over filling, pressing firmly. **4. Bake** at 400° for 10 minutes or until tortillas are crisp and cheese melts. Cut each quesadilla into 4 wedges. Serve with salsa and sour cream, if desired. **Yield:** 4 servings (serving size: 4 wedges and 2 tablespoons salsa).

CALORIES 288; FAT 9.7g (sat 3.6g, mono 0.1g, poly 0.2g); PROTEIN 12.9g; CARB 35.7g; FIBER 4.1g; CHOL 20mg; IRON 2mg; SODIUM 515mg; CALC 419mg

"It was so good, and I want my mom to make those on Sunday Mexican night at our house. The best—I loved it!"

Jarrett, age 9

Making Healthy Lunchroom Choices

Hamburgers, burritos, chocolate milk—food from a school cafeteria at times looks more like fast food. But the truth is that school meals are supposed to meet recommendations from dietary guidelines, and most hot school meals are nutritionally sound. However, the growing selection of à la carte items and vending machines often tempts kids away from choosing a balanced meal. Here's how you can help your child make better food choices in the cafeteria.

❶ **Guide.** The school cafeteria is the first time most kids have sole responsibility for their meal choices, so educating kids on how to make smart choices is important. Encourage them to choose a fruit, vegetable, and dairy food at each meal. Or have them focus on getting a rainbow of colors on their plate. This naturally encourages a variety of choices at home as well as at school.

❷ **Plan.** At the start of each week, sit down with your child and look at the food options available at school. Help your child decide what he will pick, and guide his decision-making by explaining why he needs those healthier items. Although your child may not make all the choices you suggest, he will make some.

❸ **Model.** The best way to get children to make healthy food choices is to have them see you making good choices. Serving nutritious foods at meals and snacks makes children more apt to choose these same foods when they are away from home.

Canadian Bacon and Pineapple Mini Pizzas

With preshredded cheese, pineapple tidbits, and prepared pizza sauce, the only thing adults need to be responsible for is chopping the bacon and baking the pizzas. For a pepperoni pizza variation that requires no chopping, use 8 ounces miniature pepperoni slices in place of the Canadian bacon and pineapple.

Young Chefs can:

- Top muffin halves with pineapple and bacon
- Sprinkle cheese

Older Chefs can:

- Split muffins, and place on baking sheet
- Spread sauce on muffin halves

6   whole-wheat English muffins, split and toasted
¾   cup bottled pizza sauce
1   (8-ounce) can pineapple tidbits in juice, drained
6   (½-ounce) slices Canadian bacon, diced
1½   cups (6 ounces) preshredded part-skim
     mozzarella cheese

1. Preheat oven to 425°. **2. Place** muffin halves on a baking sheet. Spread each muffin half with 1 table-spoon sauce. Sprinkle pineapple and Canadian bacon evenly over sauce. Sprinkle evenly with cheese.
3. Bake at 425° for 12 minutes or until cheese is lightly browned. **Yield:** 6 servings (serving size: 2 pizzas).

CALORIES 241; FAT 6.5g (sat 3.2g, mono 1.7g, poly 0.2g); PROTEIN 16.3g; CARB 30.5g; FIBER 3.7g; CHOL 25mg; IRON 1.9mg; SODIUM 768mg; CALC 293mg

Dinner

Reconnecting around the family dinner table

Dinner

Eating dinner together as a family used to be a daily event; it was a time to slow down and catch up on the day's events with loved ones. Today, increased workloads and activities make it hard for families to meet at the dinner table. This chapter is designed to help you create quick, healthful dinners that everyone will eat so that you can get to the table and focus on what's really important—your family!

Maple Grilled Salmon

Salmon is an excellent source of high-quality protein as well as omega-3 fatty acids that are essential for brain development and heart health.

Young Chefs can:

- Hold zip-top plastic bag while liquid ingredients are added
- Sprinkle fish with salt

Older Chefs can:

- Squeeze orange for juice
- Help measure liquid ingredients

3   tablespoons maple syrup
2   tablespoons rice vinegar
2   tablespoons fresh orange juice
4   (6-ounce) salmon fillets (1 inch thick)
Cooking spray
¼   teaspoon salt

1. **Combine** first 3 ingredients in a large heavy-duty zip-top plastic bag; add fish. Seal bag, and marinate in refrigerator 3 hours. 2. **Preheat** grill or grill pan to medium-high heat. 3. **Remove** fish from marinade, reserving marinade. Pour marinade into a small saucepan; bring to a boil. Cook until reduced to 2 tablespoons (about 3 minutes). 4. **Place** fish on grill rack or pan coated with cooking spray; grill 3 to 4 minutes on each side or until desired degree of doneness. Remove fish from grill; sprinkle evenly with salt. Serve fish with sauce. **Yield:** 4 servings (serving size: 1 fillet and 1½ teaspoons sauce).

CALORIES 317; FAT 13.3g (sat 3.1g, mono 5.8g, poly 3.2g); PROTEIN 36.2g; CARB 10.9g; FIBER 0g; CHOL 87mg; IRON 0.8mg; SODIUM 227mg; CALC 31mg

Crispy Oven-Baked Fish Sticks ✛ lower-fat macaroni and cheese ✛

Crispy Oven-Baked Fish Sticks

Fresh and free of additives, this kid-friendly entrée is a healthy choice, especially when compared to its frozen commercial counterparts.

Young Chefs can:

• Mix breadcrumb ingredients
• Help pat dry fish

Older Chefs can:

• Measure breadcrumbs
• Beat egg
• Place fish in flour, egg, and then breadcrumb mixture

¾	cup whole-wheat panko (Japanese breadcrumbs)
1	tablespoon grated fresh Parmesan cheese
1	teaspoon grated lemon rind
Cooking spray	
1	pound skinless Pacific cod or other firm white fish fillets
¼	teaspoon salt
¼	teaspoon freshly ground black pepper
2	tablespoons all-purpose flour
1	large egg, beaten

1. Preheat oven to 450°. **2. Combine** first 3 ingredients in a shallow dish. Coat a wire rack with cooking spray; place on a baking sheet. **3. Cut** fish into 16 (3 x 1-inch) pieces. Rinse fish; pat dry with paper towels. Sprinkle fish evenly with salt and pepper. Place flour and egg in separate shallow dishes. Dredge 1 piece of fish in flour, shaking off any excess. Dip fish in egg; dredge in breadcrumb mixture. Repeat procedure with remaining fish, flour, egg, and breadcrumb mixture. Coat fish with cooking spray. Arrange fish on prepared wire rack. **4. Bake** at 450° for 8 minutes or until desired degree of doneness. **Yield:** 4 servings (serving size: 4 fish sticks).

CALORIES 186; FAT 2.9g (sat 0.8g, mono 0.9g, poly 0.6g); PROTEIN 25g; CARB 13.8g; FIBER 1.7g; CHOL 96mg; IRON 1.3mg; SODIUM 280mg; CALC 30mg

nutrition note

Safety First

Remember to always wash your hands well after touching raw meat, fish, poultry, or eggs, as well as to clean surfaces and utensils that have touched these foods to prevent the spread of harmful bacteria. Some tasks for kids in this chapter may involve touching raw meat, fish, poultry, or eggs, so make sure kids follow these same guidelines to keep food—and people—safe.

Shrimp "Fried" Rice

Many take-out versions can be heavy in fat and low in nutrients. This entrée, featuring brown rice, is a quick and healthful alternative to take-out.

Young Chefs can:

- Measure frozen peas
- Pour soy sauce mixture over rice

Older Chefs can:

- Beat eggs
- Help peel shrimp
- Help chop green onions with assistance

3   (3½-ounce) bags boil-in-bag brown rice
Cooking spray
2   large eggs, lightly beaten
1   tablespoon canola oil
12 ounces medium shrimp, peeled and deveined
3   tablespoons lower-sodium soy sauce
2   tablespoons rice vinegar
1   teaspoon dark sesame oil
¼   teaspoon salt
1   cup chopped green onions
1   tablespoon bottled minced fresh
    ginger
2   cups frozen petite green peas

1. Cook rice according to package directions, omitting salt and fat; drain. Remove rice from bags; return to pan. Cover and keep warm. **2. While rice cooks,** heat a large nonstick skillet over medium-high heat. Coat pan with cooking spray. Add eggs to pan; cook 1 minute or until set. Remove eggs from pan; coarsely chop. Return pan to heat; add canola oil. Add shrimp; cook 2 minutes, stirring often. **3. While shrimp cook,** combine soy sauce and next 3 ingredients in a small bowl. **4. Add** onions and ginger to shrimp; sauté 1 minute. Add peas, stirring until thoroughly heated. Stir shrimp mixture and egg into rice, and drizzle with soy sauce mixture. Fluff well with a fork, and serve immediately.

Yield: 6 servings (serving size: about 1⅓ cups).

CALORIES 335; FAT 7.2g (sat 1g, mono 2.6g, poly 1.7g); PROTEIN 21.1g; CARB 46.9g; FIBER 5g; CHOL 157mg; IRON 3.4mg; SODIUM 583mg; CALC 85mg

Grilled Vegetables and Chickpeas with Couscous

Served with couscous, the veggie-bean combination makes a complete one-dish meal with rich flavors of the Middle East. Substitute Parmesan cheese for feta if you would like a milder cheese.

Young Chefs can:

- Gather produce
- Drain and rinse beans in strainer

Older Chefs can:

- Halve tomatoes with adult supervision
- Crumble and sprinkle cheese

1   large zucchini (about 8 ounces)
1   large yellow squash (about 6 ounces)
1   small green bell pepper, seeded and quartered
1   small red bell pepper, seeded and quartered
1   small onion, cut into ¼-inch-thick slices
     (about 1 cup)
Cooking spray
1   cup water
½   cup uncooked couscous
¾   cup cherry or grape tomatoes, halved
2   tablespoons chopped fresh cilantro
3   tablespoons fresh lemon juice
1   tablespoon extra-virgin olive oil
¼   teaspoon salt
¼   teaspoon ground cumin
Dash of ground cinnamon
1   (16-ounce) can chickpeas (garbanzo beans),
     rinsed and drained
¼   cup (1 ounce) crumbled feta cheese

1. Preheat grill to medium-high heat. **2. Cut** zucchini and yellow squash lengthwise into ¼-inch-thick slices; coat squashes, bell peppers, and onion with cooking spray. Place vegetables on grill rack coated with cooking spray; grill 3 minutes on each side or until well browned. Remove vegetables to a cutting board; let cool. Chop bell peppers and onion into bite-sized pieces; place in a large bowl. **3. While vegetables cook,** bring 1 cup water to a boil in a medium sauce-pan; gradually stir in couscous. Remove from heat; cover and let stand 5 minutes. Fluff with a fork.
4. Add couscous, tomatoes, and next 7 ingredients to vegetable mixture; toss well. Sprinkle each serving with cheese. **Yield:** 4 servings (serving size: 1½ cups couscous mixture and 1 tablespoon cheese).

CALORIES 245; FAT 6.6g (sat 1.7g, mono 3.4g, poly 0.9g); PROTEIN 9.1g; CARB 39g; FIBER 6.7g; CHOL 6mg; IRON 1.7mg; SODIUM 333mg; CALC 86mg

GI Joes

This meatless take on sloppy joes uses soy crumbles, which can be found in the frozen food section of most grocery stores.

Young Chefs can:

- Watch tomatoes rehydrate
- Measure chopped bell pepper

Older Chefs can:

- Measure brown sugar
- Place buns on plate, and help assemble sandwiches

1	cup boiling water
½	cup sun-dried tomatoes, packed without oil
1	tablespoon olive oil
1½	cups chopped onion
1	cup chopped red bell pepper
2	garlic cloves, minced
¼	cup packed brown sugar
1	teaspoon dried oregano
1	teaspoon chili powder
2	teaspoons lower-sodium Worcestershire sauce
½	teaspoon ground cumin
½	teaspoon black pepper
⅛	teaspoon salt
1	(28-ounce) can crushed tomatoes, undrained
1	(12-ounce) package frozen meatless recipe crumbles
8	(1.8-ounce) white-wheat hamburger buns

1. Combine 1 cup boiling water and sun-dried tomatoes in a small bowl; let stand 15 minutes. Drain. **2. While tomatoes hydrate,** heat oil in a large nonstick skillet over medium-high heat. Add onion, bell pepper, and garlic. Cook 6 minutes or until vegetables are tender, stirring frequently. Stir in sun-dried tomatoes, brown sugar, and next 7 ingredients. Bring to a boil; reduce heat to medium-low, and simmer, uncovered, 6 minutes or until slightly thick, stirring occasionally. **3. Stir** meatless crumbles into vegetable mixture; cook over medium-high heat 4 minutes or until thoroughly heated, stirring frequently. **4. Spoon** about ½ cup vegetable mixture onto each bun bottom; cover with bun tops. **Yield:** 8 servings (serving size: 1 sandwich).

CALORIES 267; FAT 6.2g (sat 0.8g, mono 1.7g, poly 2.6g); PROTEIN 15.6g; CARB 45.8g; FIBER 10.9g; CHOL 0mg; IRON 6.1mg; SODIUM 660mg; CALC 313mg

nutrition note
Where's the Meat?

Several recipes like GI Joes, Grilled Vegetables and Chickpeas with Couscous (page 69), and Pasta with Winter Squash and Pine Nuts (page 72) derive their protein from whole grains, beans, vegetables, and nuts, rather than from meat and poultry. But these recipes aren't just for vegetarians. Dietary guidelines recommend that people of all ages strive to incorporate more fish- and plant-based meals in place of animal-based meals that feature beef and chicken.

Substituting whole grains, beans, or fish for meat and poultry usually means one consumes *fewer* calories and *less* saturated fat and cholesterol, but *more* fiber, vitamins, and minerals. Research has suggested that these types of dietary changes may make an individual have less body fat and be at lower risk for heart disease, some cancers, and type 2 diabetes.

You don't have to totally give up hamburgers and chicken breasts—just strive to have meatless meals a few times per week. If you have a meat-loving family, start small by preparing one dinner a week that's fish- or plant-based, and then slowly incorporate a few more over the next few weeks.

"I totally like this recipe! I love how it tastes like lasagna."

Nathan, age 6

Easy Meatless Manicotti

Simple and cheesy—words both parents and kids love—are the best way to describe this Italian dish. Serve with a tossed salad or cut-up fruit.

Young Chefs can:

- Pour pasta sauce into bottom of dish
- Measure cheese
- Count out shells

Older Chefs can:

- Help squeeze cheese mixture into shells
- Arrange shells in pan
- Pour sauce over shells, and sprinkle with cheese

1   (26-ounce) jar tomato-basil pasta sauce, divided
1   cup water
Cooking spray
2   cups (8 ounces) shredded part-skim mozzarella cheese, divided
¼   cup (1 ounce) grated fresh Parmesan cheese
1½ teaspoons dried oregano
¼   teaspoon black pepper
1   (16-ounce) carton fat-free cottage cheese
1   (10-ounce) package frozen chopped spinach, thawed, drained, and squeezed dry
1   (8-ounce) package manicotti (14 shells), uncooked

1. Preheat oven to 375°. **2. Combine** pasta sauce and 1 cup water. Pour half of pasta sauce mixture into a 13 x 9-inch glass or ceramic baking dish coated with cooking spray. **3. Combine** 1¼ cups mozzarella, Parmesan cheese, and next 4 ingredients. Spoon mixture into a heavy-duty zip-top plastic bag; snip off 1 corner of bag. Squeeze about 3 tablespoons cheese mixture into each uncooked pasta shell. Arrange stuffed shells in a single layer over sauce mixture; pour remaining sauce mixture over shells. Top with remaining ¾ cup mozzarella. Cover tightly with foil. **4. Bake** at 375° for 1 hour or until shells are tender. Let stand 10 minutes before serving. **Yield:** 7 servings (serving size: 2 manicotti).

CALORIES 335; FAT 9.2g (sat 5g, mono 3.1g, poly 0.5g); PROTEIN 23.8g; CARB 39.2g; FIBER 4g; CHOL 26mg; IRON 2.6mg; SODIUM 827mg; CALC 453mg

Pasta with Winter Squash and Pine Nuts

Squash is the main ingredient in this pasta, but you would never know it. This vegetable gives the sauce a thick, creamy texture. Make sure to cook the squash until it's very tender.

Young Chefs can:

- Add sugar, salt, and pepper to squash
- Sprinkle pasta with cheese

Older Chefs can:

- Help mash squash
- Sauté pine nuts with adult supervision

1	pound butternut squash, peeled, seeded, and cut into 1-inch cubes
12	ounces uncooked whole-wheat penne rigate
2	tablespoons butter
¼	cup pine nuts
1	garlic clove, minced
1	tablespoon chopped fresh sage
1	teaspoon sugar
¾	teaspoon salt
¼	teaspoon black pepper
1	cup (4 ounces) grated fresh Parmesan cheese

1. Cook squash in boiling water to cover in a large saucepan 15 minutes or until tender; drain. Mash squash with a potato masher until smooth. **2. While squash cooks,** cook pasta in a large Dutch oven according to package directions, omitting salt and fat; drain and return to pan. **3. Melt** butter in a small nonstick skillet over medium heat; add pine nuts and garlic. Cook, stirring frequently, 2 to 3 minutes or until pine nuts are lightly browned. Remove from heat, and stir in sage. **4. Stir** sugar, salt, and pepper into mashed squash. Stir squash mixture and pine nut mixture into hot pasta. Sprinkle with cheese. Serve immediately.

Yield: 6 servings (serving size: 1 cup).

CALORIES 374; FAT 15.2g (sat 6g, mono 3.6g, poly 3.8g); PROTEIN 16g; CARB 52.8g; FIBER 7.8g; CHOL 27mg; IRON 2.9mg; SODIUM 610mg; CALC 271mg

kitchen classroom

Mealtime History

Did you ever wonder how eating three meals a day came about? Though specifics differ among cultures and time periods, meals during the 17th and 18th centuries usually consisted of a breakfast, a dinner, and a supper. Breakfast was a big meal eaten as soon as one woke. It was named "breakfast" because it broke the fast one had been on while asleep. Dinner was the largest meal and was often eaten around noon. It was similar to what we now call lunch. Supper was the smallest meal, often just a snack, eaten just before dark.

Though eating a large "dinner" in the middle of the day and having just a snack at night may seem odd to us, our ancestors may have been years ahead of us from a health perspective. Eating a larger meal midday, which would be our lunch, makes logical sense so that one has plenty of energy to get through sports practices, study hall, work, and afternoon activities. A light snack just before bed also seems more appropriate than a large meal since our bodies are preparing to rest and don't need as much energy.

"I really like the shells instead of regular mac and cheese. I think I would want asparagus with this."

Parker, age 12

Baked Shells and Cheese with Cauliflower and Ham

If you have mac and cheese fans, then you'll love this baked version that incorporates cauliflower into the pasta and cheese mixture.

Young Chefs can:

- Break cauliflower into small pieces, and place in measuring cups
- Tear bread slices into quarters

Older Chefs can:

- Dice ham with dinner knife
- Sprinkle breadcrumb mixture

8	cups water
7	cups small cauliflower florets (about 1½ pounds)
¾	teaspoon salt, divided
2⅓	cups uncooked small seashell pasta
1.1	ounces all-purpose flour (about ¼ cup)
3	cups 1% low-fat milk
2	garlic cloves, minced
1	cup (4 ounces) reduced-fat shredded sharp cheddar cheese
½	cup (2 ounces) grated fresh Parmesan cheese
2	teaspoons Dijon mustard
¼	teaspoon black pepper
¾	cup diced cooked extra-lean ham (4 ounces)
Cooking spray	
2	(1-ounce) slices whole-wheat bread
2	teaspoons butter, melted

1. **Preheat** oven to 400°. 2. **Bring** 8 cups water to a boil in a large saucepan; add cauliflower and ½ teaspoon salt to boiling water, and cook 4 minutes or until tender. Remove cauliflower with a slotted spoon to a large bowl, reserving cooking liquid; set cauliflower aside. Bring cooking liquid to a rolling boil. Add pasta, and cook 6 minutes or until al dente; drain and add to cauliflower in bowl. 3. **Weigh** or lightly spoon flour into a dry measuring cup; level with a knife. Combine flour and milk in a medium saucepan, stirring well with a whisk. Stir in garlic; cook over medium-high heat until thick (about 8 minutes), stirring frequently. Remove from heat; stir in remaining ¼ teaspoon salt, cheeses, mustard, and pepper. Pour cheese sauce over cauliflower mixture; add ham, stirring to coat. Spoon cauliflower mixture into a 13 x 9-inch glass or ceramic baking dish coated with cooking spray. 4. **Tear** bread slices into quarters. Place bread in food processor; pulse 10 times or until coarse crumbs form to measure 1 cup. Combine breadcrumbs with butter; sprinkle evenly over cauliflower mixture. Bake at 400° for 20 minutes or until lightly browned. **Yield:** 8 servings (serving size: 1¼ cups).

CALORIES 309; FAT 9.1g (sat 4.7g, mono 2.7g, poly 0.5g); PROTEIN 20.3g; CARB 36.5g; FIBER 3.9g; CHOL 34mg; IRON 1.8mg; SODIUM 674mg; CALC 345mg

Spaghetti Alfredo with Roasted Asparagus

Young Chefs can:

- Trim asparagus by breaking off ends
- Break uncooked spaghetti into smaller pieces

Older Chefs can:

- Help grate and measure Parmigiano-Reggiano cheese
- Stir together pasta, asparagus, cheese mixture, and oil

2   cups 1% low-fat milk
⅓   cup (3 ounces) ⅓-less-fat cream cheese
2   tablespoons all-purpose flour
1   teaspoon salt
1   teaspoon butter
3   garlic cloves, minced
1   cup (4 ounces) grated Parmigiano-Reggiano cheese
1   pound asparagus, trimmed and cut into 2-inch pieces (about 2½ cups)
Cooking spray
16   ounces uncooked whole-wheat spaghetti
2   tablespoons olive oil

1. Preheat oven to 425°. **2. Place** first 4 ingredients in a blender; process 15 seconds or until smooth. **3. Melt** butter in a saucepan over medium-high heat. Add garlic; sauté 30 seconds. Add milk mixture to pan; cook, stirring constantly with a whisk, 5 minutes or until mixture simmers. Cook, stirring constantly with a whisk, 2 minutes or until thick. Remove from heat; stir in cheese, and cover. **4. Place** asparagus on a jelly-roll pan coated with cooking spray. Bake at 425° for 10 minutes or until browned, stirring once. **5. Cook** pasta according to package directions, omitting salt and fat; drain well. **6. Place** pasta and asparagus in a large bowl. Add cheese mixture and oil, tossing well. Serve immediately. **Yield:** 8 servings (serving size: 1 cup).

CALORIES 317; FAT 9.1g (sat 3.2g, mono 2.8g, poly 0.4g); PROTEIN 14.7g; CARB 46.5g; FIBER 10.2g; CHOL 14mg; IRON 3.2mg; SODIUM 394mg; CALC 131mg

Baked Rigatoni with Beef

Young Chefs can:

- Pour sauce and cheese into baking dish
- Top pasta mixture with cheese

Older Chefs can:

- Add pasta and beef to baking dish
- Stir ingredients together in baking dish

1   pound ground sirloin
4   cups cooked whole-wheat rigatoni (about 2½ cups uncooked pasta)
1   (26-ounce) jar tomato-basil pasta sauce
1½   cups (6 ounces) shredded part-skim mozzarella cheese, divided
Cooking spray
¼   cup (1 ounce) grated fresh Parmesan cheese

1. Preheat oven to 350°. **2. Cook** beef in a large nonstick skillet over medium-high heat until browned, stirring to crumble. Drain well. Combine beef, rigatoni, sauce, and 1 cup mozzarella cheese in an 11 x 7–inch glass or ceramic baking dish coated with cooking spray. Top with remaining ½ cup mozzarella cheese and ¼ cup Parmesan cheese. **3. Bake,** uncovered, at 350° for 20 minutes or until thoroughly heated. **Yield:** 8 servings (serving size: 1 cup).

CALORIES 276; FAT 11.5g (sat 5.1g, mono 3.7g, poly 0.3g); PROTEIN 21.7g; CARB 21.2g; FIBER 3.2g; CHOL 54mg; IRON 2.4mg; SODIUM 543mg; CALC 284mg

kitchen classroom

Dinnertime Solutions

Don't let distractions and food preferences derail your family dinners. Here are some tips to get food on the table quickly and keep family dinners enjoyable.

Make it a habit. Although you may not to do it every single day, make eating together the norm. Start when children are young, and try to eat around the same time each night so that dinner together becomes a daily event to them.

Assign tasks. From setting the table to pouring drinks, there's something for everyone to help with at dinnertime. Assigning tasks not only helps family members feel included but also teaches responsibility and eases the cook's workload.

Turn it off! Log off the computer, silence the cell phone, and turn off the TV. Eliminating distractions will help you focus on each other and your time together.

Encourage new foods. However, don't pressure your child to eat them. Foods may have to be served several times before a child will try them, so don't give

up. Also, serve new foods in small portions to appear less overwhelming, and only offer one new food at a time.

Ask questions. Engage your kids in conversation by asking about their day—what they learned at school, what they ate for lunch, what part of their day was their favorite. Keep the conversation fun and happy.

Serve one meal. Prepare the same foods for everyone, but give your child a voice. Parents shouldn't be short-order cooks, so plan your meal around family preferences and stick to it. But give your child a little bit of control when possible, such as asking if he would prefer the carrot or the broccoli that you prepared—or both!

Stock up on quick basics. Keeping your pantry stocked with foods you can quickly throw together will make having family dinners easier on busier days. Some quick food ideas are whole-wheat pasta, brown rice, beans, pasta sauce, whole-wheat tortillas, frozen skinless chicken breasts, and frozen vegetables.

"This recipe was very flavorful and had a great spread."

Ella, age 10

Mini-Hamburgers with Shallot-Dijon Spread

These mini-burgers are perfect for small hands. The tangy shallot mixture received a thumbs-up from our Kids Taste-Testing Panel, but feel free to stick with ketchup and mustard if your kids prefer that.

Young Chefs can:

• Pull apart dinner rolls
• Count out 16 pickle chips

Older Chefs can:

• Stir together shallot mixture
• Assemble burgers

1	pound ground sirloin
½	teaspoon kosher salt
¼	teaspoon freshly ground black pepper
Cooking spray	
3	tablespoons finely chopped shallots
1	tablespoon Worcestershire sauce
1	tablespoon Dijon mustard
2	teaspoons butter, softened
1	(8-ounce) package classic dinner rolls
16	dill pickle chips

1. Preheat grill to medium-high heat. **2. Combine** first 3 ingredients in a bowl. Divide meat mixture into 8 equal portions, shaping each into a ¼-inch-thick patty. Lightly coat both sides of patties with cooking spray. Place patties on grill rack; grill for 3 minutes on each side or until done. **3. Combine** shallots, Worcestershire sauce, mustard, and butter in a small bowl. Cut rolls in half horizontally. Spread shallot mixture evenly over cut sides of rolls. Layer 1 patty and 2 pickle chips on bottom half of each roll; top with roll tops. **Yield:** 8 servings (serving size: 1 hamburger).

CALORIES 169; FAT 5.4g (sat 2g, mono 1.8g, poly 1g); PROTEIN 14.2g; CARB 16.2g; FIBER 0.6g; CHOL 34mg; IRON 2.1mg; SODIUM 538mg; CALC 55mg

Yankee Pot Roast with Winter Vegetables

If you have a picky eater, try serving this with a slotted spoon to eliminate the liquid; then make sure to separate the meat from vegetables on the plate.

Young Chefs can:

- Measure rutabaga, parsnip, carrot, and potato
- Place rutabaga, parsnip, carrot, and potato in slow cooker

Older Chefs can:

- Measure mustard, thyme, and sage
- Help pour broth mixture into slow cooker

2½ cups (1½-inch) cubed peeled rutabaga (about 1 pound)
2½ cups (1½-inch) cubed peeled parsnip (about 1 pound)
2 cups (1½-inch) cubed peeled baking potato (about 1 pound)
1½ cups (1½-inch-thick) slices carrot (about 8 ounces)
1 teaspoon canola oil
1 (3-pound) sirloin tip roast, trimmed
Cooking spray
1 cup chopped onion
2 cups fat-free, lower-sodium beef broth
1 tablespoon whole-grain Dijon mustard
1 teaspoon salt
1 teaspoon dried thyme
½ teaspoon freshly ground black pepper
½ teaspoon dried sage
2 bay leaves
Fresh thyme sprigs (optional)

⊹⊹⊹⊹⊹⊹ kitchen classroom ⊹⊹⊹⊹⊹⊹
Root Vegetables

I f you're hesitant to try this recipe because rutabagas and parsnips aren't common vegetables in your house, don't be. Rutabagas, parsnips, carrots, and potatoes are all considered root vegetables that grow deep in the soil. Their starchy nature provides a hint of sweetness to dishes when cooked which often appeals to both kids and adults. In addition, root vegetables are great sources of Vitamin C and fiber.

1. Place first 4 ingredients in a 5-quart electric slow cooker; toss gently. **2. Heat** oil in a large skillet over medium-high heat. Add beef to pan, browning on all sides (about 8 minutes). Place beef over vegetables in slow cooker. Coat skillet with cooking spray. Add onion to pan; sauté 5 minutes or until onion begins to brown. Stir in broth, scraping pan to loosen browned bits. Reduce heat; stir in mustard and next 5 ingredients. Pour broth mixture over beef and vegetables. **3. Cover** and cook on LOW 8 hours or until beef and vegetables are very tender. Discard bay leaves. Garnish with thyme sprigs, if desired. **Yield:** 8 servings (serving size: about 4 ounces beef and 1 cup vegetables).

CALORIES 410; FAT 14.3g (sat 4.9g, mono 7g, poly 0.9g); PROTEIN 38.6g; CARB 31.2g; FIBER 6.5g; CHOL 99mg; IRON 3.7mg; SODIUM 490mg; CALC 112mg

Greek Pasta with Meatballs

This take-off on spaghetti and meatballs uses rice-shaped pasta, ground lamb, and feta cheese. Some kids may prefer a milder cheese such as shredded mozzarella. Break apart the meatballs before serving to younger children to make the meatballs easier to eat.

Young Chefs can:

- Add measured breadcrumbs
- Sprinkle meatballs with cheese

Older Chefs can:

- Help shape meatballs
- Pour marinara over meatballs

⅓	cup dry breadcrumbs
½	teaspoon dried oregano
¼	teaspoon ground cinnamon
¼	teaspoon freshly ground black pepper
1	pound lean ground lamb
1	garlic clove, minced
2	tablespoons chopped fresh parsley, divided
2	large egg whites
1½	teaspoons olive oil
2	cups bottled marinara sauce
¾	cup (3 ounces) crumbled feta cheese
2	cups hot cooked orzo

1. Preheat oven to 375°. **2. Combine** breadcrumbs, next 5 ingredients, and 1½ tablespoons parsley in a medium bowl. Add egg whites, stirring mixture until just combined. Shape mixture into 12 (1½-inch) meatballs; cover and chill meatballs 5 minutes. **3. Heat** oil in a large ovenproof skillet over medium-high heat. Add meatballs to pan; cook 8 minutes, turning to brown on all sides. Drain well; wipe pan clean with paper towels. Return meatballs to pan. Spoon marinara sauce over meatballs; sprinkle with cheese. Bake at 375° for 12 to 13 minutes or until meatballs are done. Sprinkle with remaining 1½ teaspoons parsley. Serve over orzo. **Yield:** 4 servings (serving size: ½ cup orzo, 3 meatballs, and ½ cup sauce).

CALORIES 486; FAT 14.1g (sat 5.7g, mono 4.5g, poly 0.8g); PROTEIN 37.4g; CARB 50.7g; FIBER 3.9g; CHOL 94mg; IRON 5.8mg; SODIUM 774mg; CALC 164mg

"It tastes like steak!"

Adeline, age 5

Parmesan and Sage-Crusted Pork Chops

Cheese and fresh sage add robust flavors as well as a light coating to these lean chops. Set up an assembly line—flour, egg white mixture, then breadcrumb mixture—to make coating the chops a quick task.

Young Chefs can:

- Tear bread slice into pieces
- Combine measured ingredients for breadcrumb mixture

Older Chefs can:

- Tear sage leaves off stem
- Combine and whisk mustard and egg whites
- Help coat pork chops with flour, egg white mixture, and breadcrumb mixture

1	(1¼-ounce) white bread slice, torn into pieces
¼	cup (1 ounce) grated Parmigiano-Reggiano cheese
1	tablespoon chopped fresh sage
¼	teaspoon salt
¼	cup all-purpose flour
1	tablespoon prepared mustard
2	large egg whites
4	(4-ounce) boneless loin pork chops, trimmed
1½	tablespoons canola oil

1. Place bread in a food processor; pulse bread 10 times or until coarse crumbs measure about 1 cup. Combine breadcrumbs, cheese, sage, and salt in a shallow dish. Place flour in another shallow dish. Combine mustard and egg whites in another shallow dish, stirring with a whisk. **2. Working with 1 pork chop at a time,** dredge pork in flour, shaking off excess. Dip pork into egg white mixture; dredge in breadcrumb mixture. Repeat procedure with remaining pork, flour, egg white mixture, and breadcrumb mixture. **3. Heat** a large nonstick skillet over medium heat. Add oil to pan, swirling to coat. Add pork; cook 3 minutes on each side or until browned. **Yield:** 4 servings (serving size: 1 pork chop).

CALORIES 258; FAT 10.4g (sat 2g, mono 5g, poly 2.1g); PROTEIN 28.9g; CARB 10.8g; FIBER 0.6g; CHOL 79mg; IRON 1.5mg; SODIUM 349mg; CALC 58mg

meals made easy

Parmesan and Sage-Crusted Pork Chops

+

+

Creamy Two-Cheese Polenta (page 102)

"The seasoning was really good! I'd want to eat the sandwich with sweet potatoes."

Parker, age 12

Grilled Pork Tenderloin Sandwiches

Perfect for busy ballpark nights, these sandwiches are good served hot or cold. Cook pork ahead of time, and then assemble when ready to eat.

Young Chefs can:

- Stir together ranch dressing and barbecue sauce
- Place bottom bun half on plate, and top sandwich with remaining bun half

Older Chefs can:

- Brush pork with jelly
- Spread ranch dressing mixture on bun

¼   cup pepper jelly
1   tablespoon paprika
2   teaspoons brown sugar
1   teaspoon salt
1   teaspoon ground cumin
1   teaspoon chili powder
2   pounds pork tenderloin (about 3 tenderloins), trimmed
Cooking spray
¼   cup light ranch dressing
¼   cup sweet hickory smoke tomato-based barbecue sauce
8   (1½-ounce) white-wheat hamburger buns

1. Preheat grill to medium-high heat. **2. Microwave** jelly at HIGH 15 seconds or until melted. **3. Combine** paprika and next 4 ingredients; rub evenly over pork. Place pork on grill rack coated with cooking spray; cover and grill 15 minutes, turning pork occasionally. Brush pork with jelly. Grill an additional 5 minutes or until thermometer registers 160° (slightly pink). **4. Place** pork on a cutting surface. Lightly cover with foil; let stand 10 minutes. **5. While pork stands,** combine ranch dressing and barbecue sauce in a large bowl. Cut pork into thin slices. Spread 1 tablespoon dressing mixture over bottom of each bun. Place pork slices evenly over dressing, and cover with bun tops.
Yield: 8 servings (serving size: 1 sandwich).

CALORIES 265; FAT 6.1g (sat 1.4g, mono 1.4g, poly 1.9g); PROTEIN 28.5g; CARB 27.7g; FIBER 4.7g; CHOL 76mg; IRON 4mg; SODIUM 743mg; CALC 230mg

Baked Chicken Enchiladas

Loaded with veggies, this quick weeknight dinner cooks up in just 15 minutes.

Young Chefs can:

- Measure shredded zucchini
- Count out tortillas

Older Chefs can:

- Stir salsa and sour cream together
- Assemble tortillas, and place in baking dish

1	cup bottled salsa, divided
1	(8-ounce) carton light sour cream
1½	cups chopped cooked chicken breast (about ¾ pound)
⅔	cup shredded zucchini (about 1 medium)
⅔	cup chopped tomato
⅓	cup chopped green or red bell pepper
⅓	cup chopped onion
6	(7-inch) whole-wheat flour tortillas
Cooking spray	
¾	cup (3 ounces) preshredded reduced-fat 4-cheese Mexican blend cheese

1. Preheat oven to 350°. **2. Combine** ½ cup salsa and sour cream in a small bowl. Combine chicken and next 4 ingredients in a large bowl. Spread 2 tablespoons salsa mixture over each tortilla. Spoon ½ cup chicken mixture evenly down center of each tortilla; roll up. Place rolls, seam sides down, in a 13 x 9–inch glass or ceramic baking dish coated with cooking spray. Top with remaining ½ cup salsa. **3. Bake,** uncovered, at 350° for 15 minutes. Sprinkle with cheese; bake an additional 5 minutes or until cheese melts. **Yield:** 6 servings (serving size: 1 enchilada).

CALORIES 335; FAT 11.1g (sat 5g, mono 2.8g, poly 0.8g); PROTEIN 27.9g; CARB 31.9g; FIBER 4.4g; CHOL 68mg; IRON 2.5mg; SODIUM 758mg; CALC 317mg

meals made easy

Baked Chicken Enchiladas

┼

Fruit Salad with Yogurt Dressing (page 91) or

┼

fat-free or 1% low-fat milk

nutrition note

Wrap It Up

Whole-wheat tortillas are a great way to add some fun to ordinary sandwiches and snacks. Forget the bread, and try sandwich fixings like turkey, ham, cheeses, hummus, and veggies wrapped in a tortilla. Or be more adventurous with tossed salads, scrambled eggs, or peanut butter and banana slices. Opt for whole-wheat or whole-grain tortillas with 3 grams of fat or less to maximize nutrient content, and watch the size and calorie content. Some tortillas can have up to 300 calories each! Smaller whole-grain taco or fajita-size tortillas (6-inch or 7-inch) are usually perfect for kids and typically have around 130 calories and 3 to 5 grams of fiber.

Pan-Fried Chicken

Cooking in a small amount of heart-healthy peanut oil adds flavor and makes the chicken crispy.

Young chefs can:

- Shake chicken in sealed plastic bag
- Tear off and stack paper towels

Older chefs can:

- Measure flours and spices
- Add measured ingredients to plastic bag

1	cup all-purpose flour
½	cup whole-wheat flour
1	teaspoon ground ginger
½	teaspoon ground cinnamon
½	teaspoon freshly ground nutmeg
½	teaspoon fine sea salt
2	bone-in chicken breast halves (about 1¼ pounds), skinned
2	chicken thighs (about 10 ounces), skinned
2	chicken drumsticks (about 10 ounces), skinned
¼	cup peanut oil

1. Place first 5 ingredients in a large heavy-duty zip-top plastic bag. Seal bag, and shake to blend. Sprinkle salt evenly over chicken. Add chicken, 1 piece at a time, to bag. Seal bag, and shake to coat chicken. Remove chicken from bag, shaking off excess flour. Place chicken on a cooling rack; place rack in a jelly-roll pan. Reserve and refrigerate remaining flour mixture in bag. Loosely cover chicken with wax paper; chill 1½ hours.

Let chicken stand at room temperature 30 minutes. Return chicken, 1 piece at a time, to flour mixture, shaking bag to coat chicken. Discard excess flour mixture. **2. Heat** peanut oil in a large skillet over medium-high heat. Add chicken to pan. Reduce heat to medium, and cook 25 minutes or until done, carefully turning every 5 minutes. **3. Line** a clean cooling rack with several layers of paper towels. Drain chicken on paper towels; let stand 5 minutes. **Yield:** 4 servings (serving size: 1 chicken breast half or 1 thigh and 1 drumstick).

CALORIES 245; FAT 10.1g (sat 2g, mono 4.1g, poly 3g); PROTEIN 28.2g; CARB 9g; FIBER 0.8g; CHOL 87mg; IRON 1.8mg; SODIUM 240mg; CALC 17mg

Pan-Fried Chicken ✛ **steamed carrots or green beans** ✛

Almond-Crusted Chicken with Green Onion Rice

Young Chefs can:

- Shake chicken in sealed bag
- Measure almonds

Older Chefs can:

- Pound chicken
- Dredge chicken in buttermilk mixture and almond mixture.

4	(6-ounce) skinless, boneless chicken breast halves
½	teaspoon salt, divided
¼	teaspoon black pepper
¼	cup all-purpose flour
½	cup low-fat buttermilk
2	tablespoons honey mustard
⅔	cup sliced almonds
½	cup dry breadcrumbs
	Cooking spray
¼	cup chopped green onions
2	cups hot cooked brown rice

1. Preheat oven to 450°. **2. Place** chicken breasts between 2 sheets of heavy-duty plastic wrap; pound to ½-inch thickness using a meat mallet or small heavy skillet. Sprinkle chicken with ¼ teaspoon salt and ¼ teaspoon pepper. **3. Place** flour in a zip-top plastic bag. Working with 1 piece at a time, add chicken to bag; seal and shake to coat. Remove chicken from bag, shaking off excess flour. Repeat with remaining chicken. **4. Combine** buttermilk and honey mustard in a shallow bowl. Combine almonds and breadcrumbs in another shallow bowl. Dip chicken in buttermilk mixture; dredge in almond mixture. **5. Heat** a large nonstick ovenproof skillet over medium-high heat. Coat pan with cooking spray. Add chicken; cook 1 minute. Turn chicken over. Place pan in oven; bake at 450° for 13 minutes or until chicken is done. **6. Stir** remaining ¼ teaspoon salt and ¼ cup green onions into rice. Serve rice with chicken.

Yield: 4 servings (serving size: 1 chicken breast half and ½ cup rice mixture).

CALORIES 478; FAT 12.1g (sat 1.6g, mono 5.3g, poly 2.4g); PROTEIN 49.1g; CARB 44g; FIBER 4.1g; CHOL 100mg; IRON 2.4mg; SODIUM 599mg; CALC 105mg

Feta, Herb, and Sun-Dried Tomato-Stuffed Chicken

Cooking the chicken in foil makes cleanup a breeze, and kids love having their own chicken "packet."

Young Chefs can:

- Pull basil and oregano leaves off stems
- Sprinkle lemon rind on stuffed chicken breasts

Older Chefs can:

- Combine stuffing ingredients
- Fold and crimp packets closed, and place on baking sheet

½   cup julienne-cut sun-dried tomatoes, packed without oil
½   cup (2 ounces) crumbled feta cheese
2   teaspoons chopped fresh basil
1   teaspoon chopped fresh oregano
½   teaspoon minced garlic
¼   teaspoon freshly ground black pepper
4   (6-ounce) skinless, boneless chicken breast halves
¼   teaspoon kosher salt
2   tablespoons butter
½   teaspoon grated lemon rind
¼   cup fat-free, lower-sodium chicken broth

1. Preheat oven to 425°. **2. Combine** first 6 ingredients in a small bowl. **3. Cut** a horizontal slit through 1 side of each chicken breast half to form a deep pocket. Stuff ¼ cup tomato mixture into each pocket. Sprinkle both sides of chicken evenly with salt. **4. Fold** 4 (16 x 12-inch) sheets of heavy-duty foil in half crosswise. Open foil; place 1½ teaspoons butter on half of each foil sheet. Place 1 stuffed chicken breast half on top of each portion of butter. Sprinkle ⅛ teaspoon grated lemon rind on top of each stuffed chicken breast half, and drizzle each serving with 1 tablespoon chicken broth. Fold foil over chicken, and tightly crimp edges. Place packets on a rimmed baking sheet. **5. Bake** at 425° for 20 minutes. Remove from oven, and let stand for 5 minutes. Carefully open packets; transfer each chicken breast half to a serving plate. Cut each chicken breast half crosswise into ½-inch-thick slices. Serve immediately. **Yield:** 4 servings (serving size: 1 stuffed chicken breast half).

CALORIES 295; FAT 11.1g (sat 6.4g, mono 2.7g, poly 0.9g); PROTEIN 42.4g; CARB 4.8g; FIBER 1g; CHOL 127mg; IRON 2mg; SODIUM 599mg; CALC 103mg

meals made easy

Feta, Herb, and Sun-Dried Tomato–Stuffed Chicken

+

whole-wheat pasta tossed with olive oil

+

Grilled Asparagus Rafts (page 92) or

Chicago Deep-Dish Pizza

The whole family is happy when it's pizza night. This version features chicken sausage, but feel free to substitute another lean meat topping like turkey pepperoni or Canadian bacon.

Young Chefs can:

- Measure cheese
- Measure mushrooms and chopped bell peppers

Older Chefs can:

- Chop sausage with dinner knife
- Help press dough into baking dish

2   teaspoons sugar
1   package dry yeast (about 2¼ teaspoons)
1   cup warm water (100° to 110°)
12.4 ounces all-purpose flour (about 2¾ cups) plus 2 tablespoons, divided
¼   cup yellow cornmeal
½   teaspoon salt
1   tablespoon extra-virgin olive oil
Cooking spray
1   (28-ounce) can whole tomatoes, drained
1½   teaspoons chopped fresh oregano
1½   teaspoons chopped fresh basil
2   cups thinly sliced mushrooms (about 6 ounces)
¾   cup chopped green bell pepper
¾   cup chopped red bell pepper
2   cups (8 ounces) shredded part-skim mozzarella cheese, divided
2   precooked mild Italian chicken sausages (about 6 ounces), casings removed and chopped

1. Dissolve sugar and yeast in 1 cup warm water in a large bowl; let stand 5 minutes. **2. Weigh** or lightly spoon 12.4 ounces flour (about 2¾ cups) into dry measuring cups; level with a knife. Combine 9 ounces flour (about 2 cups), cornmeal, and salt in a bowl. Stir oil into yeast mixture; stir in flour mixture. Add remaining 3.4 ounces flour (about ¾ cup) to form a soft dough. Turn dough out onto a lightly floured surface. Knead until smooth and elastic (about 5 minutes); add enough of remaining 2 tablespoons flour, 1 tablespoon at a time, to prevent dough from sticking to hands (dough will feel sticky). **3. Place** dough in a large bowl coated with cooking spray, turning to coat top. Cover and let rise in a warm place (85°), free from drafts, 45 minutes or until doubled in size. (Gently press two fingers into dough. If indentation remains, dough has risen enough.) **4. Preheat** oven to 400°. **5. Punch** dough down; cover and let rest 5 minutes. Roll dough into an 11 x 15–inch rectangle on a lightly floured surface. Place dough in a 13 x 9–inch glass or ceramic baking dish coated with cooking spray; press dough up sides of dish. Bake at 400° for 10 minutes. **6. While crust bakes,** chop tomatoes; place in a sieve. Drain tomato mixture 10 minutes. Pat tomatoes dry with paper towels. Place tomatoes in a large bowl; stir in oregano and basil. **7. While tomatoes drain,** heat a large nonstick skillet over medium heat. Coat pan with cooking spray. Add mushrooms to pan; cook 5 minutes without stirring. Stir in bell peppers; cook 5 minutes or until tender, stirring often. **8. Spread** 1½ cups cheese over dough, pressing gently. Arrange chopped sausage evenly over cheese. Arrange vegetables over sausage; spoon tomato mixture evenly over vegetables and sausage. Sprinkle evenly with remaining ½ cup cheese. **9. Bake** at 400° for 25 minutes or until crust browns and cheese is golden. Cool 5 minutes before cutting.

Yield: 8 servings (serving size: 1 piece).

CALORIES 339; FAT 8.9g (sat 3.7g, mono 3.5g, poly 0.9g); PROTEIN 17.4g; CARB 47.1g; FIBER 3.5g; CHOL 34mg; IRON 3.1mg; SODIUM 645mg; CALC 244mg

"I liked the burgers, especially the onions. I would eat this with French fries."

Piper, age 10

Quick-and-Easy Teriyaki Turkey Burgers

Teriyaki sauce, ginger, and sesame oil add just the right amount of flavor to these savory burgers that cook quickly in a skillet. Omit sautéed onions on the burgers for your pickier eaters.

Young Chefs can:

• Add measured garlic powder and ginger to turkey
• Place buns on plates

Older Chefs can:

▪ Help shape patties
▪ Top burgers with tomato, lettuce, and remaining bun half

1   pound ground turkey breast
2   teaspoons garlic powder
1   teaspoon bottled minced ginger
¼   teaspoon black pepper
3   tablespoons lower-sodium teriyaki sauce
1   tablespoon water
Cooking spray
1   large onion, cut into ¼-inch-thick slices (about 2 cups)
1   teaspoon dark sesame oil
4   (1½-ounce) hamburger buns
4   (¼-inch-thick) slices tomato
4   curly leaf lettuce leaves

1. Combine first 4 ingredients in a large bowl. Shape turkey mixture into 4 (½-inch-thick) patties. Combine teriyaki sauce and 1 tablespoon water in a small bowl.
2. Heat a large nonstick skillet over medium-high heat. Coat pan with cooking spray. Add onion to pan; cover and cook 7 minutes or until golden brown, stirring frequently. Stir in 1 tablespoon teriyaki mixture. Remove onion from pan; keep warm. Reduce heat to medium.
3. Coat pan with cooking spray. Add oil to pan. Add patties, and cook 5 minutes. Add remaining 3 tablespoons teriyaki mixture to pan. Carefully turn patties over, and cook 2 minutes or until done. **4. Place** 1 patty on bottom half of each bun; top each with ¼ cup onion mixture, 1 tomato slice, and 1 lettuce leaf. Top with remaining bun halves. **Yield:** 4 servings (serving size: 1 burger).

CALORIES 364; FAT 12.8g (sat 3.2g, mono 4.5g, poly 3.7g); PROTEIN 26.5g; CARB 35g; FIBER 3.3g; CHOL 90mg; IRON 3.7mg; SODIUM 660mg; CALC 108mg

meals made easy

**Quick-and-Easy Teriyaki
Turkey Burgers**

+

yogurt

+

Jerk-Seasoned Turkey with Black Beans and Yellow Rice

Stir the black beans into the rice just before serving so there's less chance of discoloration.
For an extra pop of color and flavor, serve with a side of commercial peach salsa.

Young Chefs can:

- Drain and rinse beans in strainer
- Sprinkle seasoning mixture over turkey

Older Chefs can:

- Measure uncooked rice
- Help stir beans and cilantro into rice

4	teaspoons salt-free Jamaican jerk seasoning for chicken and fish, divided
¾	teaspoon salt, divided
2	(¾-pound) turkey tenderloins
4	teaspoons olive oil, divided
	Cooking spray
3	cups finely chopped onion (about 1½ large)
1	cup uncooked basmati rice
¼	teaspoon ground turmeric
2	cups fat-free, lower-sodium chicken broth
½	cup water
1	(15-ounce) can black beans, rinsed and drained
3	tablespoons chopped fresh cilantro

1. Preheat oven to 400°. **2. Combine** 1 tablespoon jerk seasoning and ½ teaspoon salt; sprinkle evenly over both sides of turkey. **3. Heat** 1 teaspoon oil in a large nonstick skillet over medium-high heat. Add turkey to pan; cook 4 minutes on each side or until browned. Place turkey on a rack in a broiler pan coated with cooking spray. Bake at 400° for 30 minutes or until a thermometer registers 165°. Remove turkey from oven; cover loosely, and let stand 5 minutes. Cut turkey across grain into thin slices. **4. While turkey cooks,** heat remaining 1 tablespoon oil in pan over medium-high heat. Add onion to pan, and sauté 8 minutes or until tender. Stir in rice, remaining 1 teaspoon jerk seasoning, and turmeric; sauté 2 minutes. Add broth, ½ cup water, and remaining ¼ teaspoon salt; bring to a boil. Cover, reduce heat, and simmer 15 minutes or until rice is tender and liquid is absorbed. Stir in beans and cilantro. Serve rice mixture with turkey. **Yield:** 6 servings (serving size: 3 ounces turkey and 1 cup rice mixture).

CALORIES 267; FAT 5.1g (sat 1g, mono 2.6g, poly 1g); PROTEIN 32.2g; CARB 27.2g; FIBER 4.2g; CHOL 45mg; IRON 2.3mg; SODIUM 654mg; CALC 34mg

"The turkey is my favorite!"
Anna, age 6

The page has a decorative background with "kid tested • kid approved" text in a circular arrangement around a star logo.
Sides

Healthy ways to round out meals

Sides

Coming up with new sides can be a challenge—especially if you have kids who'd prefer to just skip the veggies altogether. However, continuously offering a variety of foods to your child is important, and introducing new side dishes that include whole grains, fruits, vegetables, and low-fat dairy foods is a great way to do this.

Simple Salad with Ranch-Salsa Dressing

This basic salad with homemade dressing is a great way to introduce children to fresh salad greens. Store extra dressing in an airtight container in the refrigerator for up to 2 weeks.

Young Chefs can:

- Tear lettuces
- Combine measured lettuces, tomatoes, and carrots

Older Chefs can:

- Measure first 8 ingredients, and add to blender
- Halve cherry tomatoes with dinner knife

1	cup low-fat buttermilk
½	cup bottled chunky mild salsa
3	tablespoons light mayonnaise
2	tablespoons chopped fresh parsley
1	tablespoon fresh lemon juice
½	teaspoon sugar
¼	teaspoon dry mustard
¼	teaspoon salt
3	cups torn iceberg lettuce
3	cups torn romaine lettuce
1	cup cherry tomatoes, halved
½	cup sliced carrot
3	tablespoons sliced green onions

1. Place first 8 ingredients in a blender; process until smooth. **2. Combine** lettuces and next 3 ingredients in a large bowl. Add ¾ cup dressing; toss well. Serve immediately. **Yield:** 7 servings (serving size: 1 cup).

CALORIES 34; FAT 1.2g (sat 0.2g, mono 0.1g, poly 0.1g); PROTEIN 1.3g; CARB 5.3g; FIBER 1.4g; CHOL 1mg; IRON 0.5mg; SODIUM 111mg; CALC 37mg

meals made easy

Spinach and Corn Quesadillas (page 61)

—+—

Simple Salad with Ranch-Salsa Dressing

—+—

Fruit Salad with Yogurt Dressing

The yogurt dressing sweetens any slightly unripe fruit and also dresses up basic fruit salad. Play around with different flavors of jam or even flavored yogurt to suit your imagination.

Young Chefs can:

- Wash apricots
- Measure blueberries

Older Chefs can:

- Halve grapes with dinner knife
- Stir fruit and yogurt mixture together

2 tablespoons plain fat-free yogurt
1 tablespoon seedless raspberry jam
1½ cups sliced peaches (about 2)
1 cup fresh blueberries
1 cup sliced apricots (about 2)
½ cup seedless green grapes (about 14), cut in half

1. Combine yogurt and jam in a small bowl. Combine peaches and next 3 ingredients in a large bowl. Add yogurt mixture to fruit, and toss gently to coat. **Yield:** 4 servings (serving size: 1 cup).

CALORIES 92; FAT 0.5g (sat 0g, mono 0.1g, poly 0.1g); PROTEIN 1.8g; CARB 22.7g; FIBER 2.7g; CHOL 0mg; IRON 0.5mg; SODIUM 5mg; CALC 22mg

"The peach was the best! I'd add some banana to it."

Julia, age 7

Grilled Asparagus Rafts

Pinning asparagus spears together with skewers makes it easier to flip them and grill evenly on both sides. Make sure to remove skewers before serving to younger children.

Young Chefs can:

- Count out and line up 4 asparagus spears
- Sprinkle grilled rafts with sesame seeds

Older Chefs can:

- Carefully thread asparagus onto skewers
- Brush rafts with soy sauce mixture before grilling

16 thick asparagus spears (about 1 pound)
1   tablespoon lower-sodium soy sauce
1   teaspoon dark sesame oil
1   garlic clove, minced
Cooking spray
2   teaspoons sesame seeds, toasted
⅛   teaspoon black pepper
Dash of salt

1. Preheat grill to high heat. **2. Snap** off tough ends of asparagus. Line up 4 asparagus spears, touching each other, on a flat surface. Thread 2 (3-inch) skewers or wooden picks horizontally through spears 1 to 1½ inches from each end to form a raft. Repeat procedure with remaining asparagus spears. **3. Combine** soy sauce, oil, and garlic, stirring with a whisk; brush evenly over rafts. Place rafts on grill rack coated with cooking spray. Grill 3 minutes on each side or until crisp-tender. Sprinkle evenly with sesame seeds, pepper, and salt. **Yield:** 4 rafts (serving size: 1 asparagus raft).

CALORIES 48; FAT 2.2g (sat 0.2g, mono 0.5g, poly 0.6g); PROTEIN 3g; CARB 5.3g; FIBER 2.4g; CHOL 0mg; IRON 4.6mg; SODIUM 190mg; CALC 29mg

Sautéed Carrots with Sage

Young Chefs can:

- Pull sage leaves off stem
- Measure cut carrots

Older Chefs can:

- Use vegetable peeler to peel carrots
- Sprinkle sage over cooked carrots

1   teaspoon butter
1   teaspoon olive oil
1½   cups (½-inch) diagonally sliced peeled carrot
         (about 4 large)
2   tablespoons water
⅛   teaspoon salt
1   teaspoon chopped fresh sage

1. Melt butter in a large nonstick skillet over medium heat. Add oil to pan; swirl to coat pan. Add carrot and 2 tablespoons water. Partially cover pan, and cook 10 minutes or until carrot is almost tender. Add salt to carrot mixture; increase heat to medium-high. Cook 4 minutes or until carrot is tender and lightly browned, stirring frequently. Sprinkle with sage. **Yield:** 2 servings (serving size: ½ cup).

CALORIES 75; FAT 4.4g (sat 1.6g, mono 2.2g, poly 0.4g); PROTEIN 0.9g; CARB 8.8g; FIBER 2.6g; CHOL 5mg; IRON 0.3mg; SODIUM 222mg; CALC 33mg

kitchen classroom

How Food Keeps You Healthy

Naturally low in calories yet high in fiber and nutrients, fruits and vegetables are some of the healthiest foods. Each fruit and vegetable offers a variety of vitamins and minerals to support growth and to keep bodies healthy. These are great short-term benefits, but did you know that eating fruits and veggies *today* may also keep you healthy in 20 or 30 years?

Antioxidants are compounds in produce that research has suggested will keep us healthy down the road. Here's how they work: Harmful particles called free radicals roam the body looking for healthy cells to damage. Antioxidants clean up free radicals by binding to them so that your body can dispose of them.

Antioxidants can only be obtained from foods—primarily fruits and vegetables. The more you get in your diet, the more protection your cells have. There's still lots to learn about how powerful antioxidants can be, but for now, the consensus is clear: Eat antioxidant-rich foods every day to stay healthy today and tomorrow.

Round Out Your Daily Intake

Side dishes are an easy way to complete your family's daily nutritional intake. Aim to eat a variety of foods—specifically fruits and vegetables—every week to get a full array of all nutrients. Here's a quick list of nutrients both kids and adults need and the foods where they are found.

Fiber: All whole grains (brown rice, wild rice, oats, whole-wheat breads and pastas), fruits, and vegetables

Iron: Beans and peas, whole grains (brown rice, oats, whole-wheat breads and pastas), spinach, turnip greens, collard greens

Potassium: All fruits and vegetables

Magnesium: Beans and peas, fat-free and low-fat milk, and milk products such as yogurt and pudding

Calcium: Broccoli, spinach, collard greens, turnip greens, beans and peas, fat-free and low-fat milk, and milk products such as yogurt and pudding

Vitamin A: Carrots, spinach, sweet potatoes, butternut squash, cantaloupe, apricots, peaches, red bell peppers, fat-free and low-fat milk

Vitamin C: Oranges and citrus fruits, kiwifruit, strawberries, bell peppers, baked potatoes, cantaloupe, tomatoes

Vitamin D: Fat-free and low-fat milk and milk products such as yogurt and pudding

Vitamin E: Spinach, broccoli, nuts, and vegetable oils

Edamame Succotash

Young Chefs can:

- Measure corn kernels and edamame
- Tear basil leaves

Older Chefs can:

- Help shuck corn
- Sprinkle bacon and basil

2	center-cut bacon slices
1½	teaspoons butter
1	cup chopped sweet onion
1	cup fresh corn kernels (about 2 ears)
1¾	cups frozen shelled edamame (green soybeans), thawed
1	cup coarsely chopped plum tomatoes (about 2 medium)
⅓	cup coarsely chopped red bell pepper
2	tablespoons fat-free half-and-half
1	tablespoon red wine vinegar
¼	teaspoon salt
¼	teaspoon sugar
2	tablespoons torn fresh basil

1. Cook bacon in a nonstick skillet over medium heat until crisp. Remove bacon from pan, reserving 2 teaspoons drippings in pan; coarsely chop bacon.

2. Increase heat to medium-high. Melt butter in drippings in pan. Add onion; sauté 3 minutes, stirring occasionally. Add corn kernels and edamame; cook 6 minutes, stirring occasionally. Stir in tomato and next 5 ingredients. Cover and cook 2 minutes or until tender. Sprinkle with bacon and basil. **Yield:** 5 servings (serving size: ½ cup).

CALORIES 158; FAT 6.4g (sat 1.7g, mono 1.2g, poly 0.5g); PROTEIN 9.6g; CARB 16.6g; FIBER 4.8g; CHOL 7mg; IRON 2.3mg; SODIUM 181mg; CALC 47mg

Spring Peas with Pancetta

Young Chefs can:

- Measure frozen peas
- Add measured peas to onion mixture with adult assistance

Older Chefs can:

- Measure broth
- Add pancetta to cooked peas

3	slices pancetta (about 1 ounce), chopped
¾	cup finely chopped onion
1	garlic clove, minced
3	cups frozen petite green peas
1	cup fat-free, lower-sodium chicken broth
¼	teaspoon salt

1. Heat a large nonstick skillet over medium-high heat. Add pancetta to pan; sauté 3 minutes or until crisp. Remove pancetta from pan, reserving drippings in pan; set pancetta aside. Add onion and garlic to drippings in pan; sauté 3 minutes or until tender. **2. Stir** peas, broth, and salt into onion mixture. Bring to a boil; reduce heat and simmer, uncovered, 6 minutes or until peas are tender, stirring occasionally. Stir in pancetta. **Yield:** 6 servings (serving size: ½ cup).

CALORIES 79; FAT 2g (sat 0.7g, mono 0.2g, poly 0.2g); PROTEIN 4.6g; CARB 11.2g; FIBER 3.4g; CHOL 3mg; IRON 1.1mg; SODIUM 323mg; CALC 20mg

Green Beans with Toasted Walnuts and Breadcrumbs

Toast fresh breadcrumbs in flavorful olive oil, and combine them with chopped toasted walnuts to add texture to this heart-healthy side dish.

Young Chefs can:

- Place shallots and green beans on baking sheet
- Tear bread slice into small pieces

Older Chefs can:

- Sprinkle green beans with salt and sugar
- Sprinkle breadcrumb mixture over green beans

½ cup sliced shallots

1 pound green beans, trimmed

Cooking spray

1 tablespoon extra-virgin olive oil, divided

¼ teaspoon salt

¼ teaspoon sugar

1 (1-ounce) French bread baguette slice, torn

2 tablespoons grated Parmigiano-Reggiano cheese

2 tablespoons chopped walnuts, toasted

1 teaspoon grated lemon rind (optional)

1. Preheat oven to 425°. **2. Place** shallots and beans on a jelly-roll pan coated with cooking spray. Drizzle bean mixture with 1½ teaspoons oil, and sprinkle with salt and sugar; toss to coat. Bake at 425° for 20 minutes or until beans are crisp-tender. Transfer mixture to a serving bowl. **3. Place** bread in a food processor; pulse 10 times or until coarse crumbs measure ¾ cup. Heat remaining 1½ teaspoons oil in a small skillet over medium heat. Add breadcrumbs to hot oil; cook 5 minutes or until golden, stirring frequently. Remove from heat; stir in cheese, walnuts, and lemon rind, if desired. Add breadcrumb mixture to bean mixture; toss well. **Yield:** 8 servings (serving size: ½ cup).

CALORIES 67; FAT 3.5g (sat 0.6g, mono 1.6g, poly 1.1g); PROTEIN 2.3g; CARB 7.7g; FIBER 1.9g; CHOL 1mg; IRON 0.8mg; SODIUM 119mg; CALC 39mg

baked fish with lemon

-|-

-|-

Green Beans with Toasted Walnuts and Breadcrumbs

Ranch Mashed Potatoes

This tasty side captures the flavor of ranch dressing without the additional calories, fat, and sodium. Make these potatoes up to one day ahead, and refrigerate until just before serving. When you reheat them, you may need to add some additional buttermilk and sour cream to achieve a rich consistency.

Young Chefs can:

- Wash potatoes
- Add measured sour cream and green onions to potatoes

Older Chefs can:

- Measure sour cream, buttermilk, and dried herbs
- Add buttermilk, butter, salt, and herbs to potatoes

6	cups cubed red potato (about 2 pounds), unpeeled
½	cup light sour cream
¼	cup chopped green onions
¼	cup low-fat buttermilk
2	tablespoons butter, softened
¾	teaspoon salt
½	teaspoon dried basil
½	teaspoon dried oregano
¼	teaspoon garlic powder
⅛	teaspoon dried dill

1. Cook potato in boiling water to cover 15 minutes or until tender; drain. Place potato in a large bowl. Add sour cream and remaining ingredients; mash with a potato masher to desired consistency. **Yield:** 10 servings (serving size: ½ cup).

CALORIES 102; FAT 3.3g (sat 2.1g, mono 0.6g, poly 0.2g); PROTEIN 2.4g; CARB 16.6g; FIBER 1.7g; CHOL 10mg; IRON 0.8mg; SODIUM 215mg; CALC 21mg

1½ cups fat-free milk
1½ tablespoons all-purpose flour
Cooking spray
½   cup thinly sliced leek
2   garlic cloves, minced
1   (16-ounce) package frozen chopped spinach, thawed, drained, and squeezed dry
¼   cup (2 ounces) ⅓-less-fat cream cheese
¼   teaspoon salt
¼   teaspoon freshly ground black pepper

1. Combine milk and flour, stirring well with a whisk.
2. Heat a medium saucepan over medium-high heat. Coat pan with cooking spray. Add leek and garlic; sauté 2 minutes or until tender. Add spinach, and sauté 1 minute. Stir in milk mixture; cook 1½ minutes or until slightly thick, stirring occasionally. **3. Add** cheese, salt, and pepper to spinach mixture in pan, stirring until smooth; cook 1 minute. **Yield:** 5 servings (serving size: ½ cup).

CALORIES 97; FAT 3.2g (sat 1.7g, mono 0g, poly 0.1g); PROTEIN 7.5g; CARB 11.4g; FIBER 2.9g; CHOL 10mg; IRON 2.1mg; SODIUM 267mg; CALC 225mg

Creamed Spinach and Leeks

This lightened classic is guaranteed to make spinach a popular vegetable around your house. This is good news since spinach is an excellent source of vitamins A and C, both of which help keep immune systems strong.

Young Chefs can:

• Measure sliced leek
• Squeeze water out of spinach

Older Chefs can:

• Combine measured milk and flour in bowl
• Measure cream cheese

Garlic Fries

Tossing the fries in butter and garlic after cooking makes them unbelievably rich and a treat for both kids and adults. Younger children may prefer the fries without the garlic mixture.

Young Chefs can:

- Place cut potatoes in zip-top plastic bag
- Shake sealed bag of potatoes

Older Chefs can:

- Use vegetable peeler to peel potatoes
- Sprinkle potatoes with cheese

1½ pounds baking potatoes, peeled and cut into ¼-inch-thick strips
2 teaspoons vegetable oil
Cooking spray
½ teaspoon salt
1 tablespoon butter
8 garlic cloves, minced (about 5 teaspoons)
2 tablespoons minced fresh parsley
2 tablespoons grated fresh Parmesan cheese

1. Preheat oven to 450°. 2. Combine potatoes and oil in a large heavy-duty zip-top plastic bag; seal bag, and toss to coat. 3. Arrange potatoes in a single layer on a baking sheet coated with cooking spray. Sprinkle with salt. Bake at 450° for 25 minutes or until potatoes are tender and golden brown, turning after 20 minutes. 4. Place butter and garlic in a large nonstick skillet; cook over low heat 4 minutes, stirring constantly. Add potatoes and parsley to butter mixture; toss to coat. Sprinkle with cheese. Serve immediately. Yield: 6 servings (serving size: ¾ cup).

CALORIES 140; FAT 4.4g (sat 1.8g, mono 1.2g, poly 0.8g); PROTEIN 3.1g; CARB 22.7g; FIBER 2g; CHOL 7mg; IRON 0.5mg; SODIUM 256mg; CALC 52mg

Maple-Roasted Acorn Squash

Made from maple syrup, maple sugar has a more intense flavor and sticks to the squash well. To save time, you can skip peeling the squash.

Young Chefs can:

- Help scoop seeds out of squash
- Stir squash to coat with sugar, oil, and salt

Older Chefs can:

- Measure and add sugar and salt
- Spoon coated squash into baking dish

3 acorn squash (about 1 pound each)
¼ cup maple sugar
1 tablespoon extra-virgin olive oil
½ teaspoon kosher salt
Cooking spray

1. Preheat oven to 425°. 2. Cut each squash in half lengthwise. Discard seeds and membranes. Cut each half crosswise into 1-inch-thick slices; peel. Combine maple sugar, oil, and salt in a large bowl. Add squash; toss to coat. 3. Place squash in a 13 x 9–inch glass or ceramic baking dish coated with cooking spray. Bake at 425° for 40 minutes or until tender, stirring every 10 minutes. Yield: 6 servings (serving size: 1 cup).

CALORIES 112; FAT 2.7g (sat 0.4g, mono 1.8g, poly 0.3g); PROTEIN 1.4g; CARB 23.4g; FIBER 2.6g; CHOL 0mg; IRON 1.3mg; SODIUM 166mg; CALC 62mg

Zucchini Oven Chips

Cheese and breadcrumbs form a crispy coating on these veggie chips. Serve with hamburgers or sandwiches in place of potato chips.

Young Chefs can:

- Combine measured breadcrumbs and cheese in bowl
- Measure zucchini

Older Chefs can:

- Coat zucchini slices with cooking spray
- Dredge zucchini slices in breadcrumb mixture

⅓	cup dry breadcrumbs
¼	cup (1 ounce) grated fresh Parmesan cheese
¼	teaspoon seasoned salt
¼	teaspoon garlic powder
⅛	teaspoon freshly ground black pepper
2½	cups (¼-inch-thick) slices zucchini (about 2 small)

Cooking spray

1. Preheat oven to 425°. **2. Combine** first 5 ingredients in a medium bowl, stirring with a whisk. Coat both sides of zucchini slices with cooking spray. Dredge zucchini slices in breadcrumb mixture, pressing gently to coat. Place coated slices on a foil-lined baking sheet coated with cooking spray. **3. Bake** at 425° for 30 minutes or until browned and crisp, turning after 15 minutes. Serve immediately. **Yield:** 4 servings (serving size: about ¾ cup).

CALORIES 71; FAT 2.4g (sat 1g, mono 0.5g, poly 0.3g); PROTEIN 3.9g; CARB 8.8g; FIBER 1.1g; CHOL 4mg; IRON 0.7mg; SODIUM 243mg; CALC 81mg

"I liked it because it made squash, which I normally hate, taste good."

Parker, age 12

Baked Couscous with Summer Squash and Herbs

Perfect for summer meals since it highlights fresh herbs and squash, this cross between a squash casserole and dressing combines your grain and vegetable all in one dish.

Young Chefs can:

- Wash squash
- Pull basil and oregano leaves off stems
- Measure cheeses

Older Chefs can:

- Measure couscous
- Help add couscous and cheese to squash mixture

1   (14.5-ounce) can fat-free, lower-sodium chicken broth, divided
1   cup uncooked couscous
Cooking spray
2   cups sliced yellow squash (about 2 small)
1   garlic clove, minced
½   cup sliced green onions
2   tablespoons chopped fresh basil
1   tablespoon chopped fresh oregano
¼   cup (1 ounce) shredded fontina cheese
¼   cup (1 ounce) grated Parmigiano-Reggiano cheese
¼   cup egg substitute
¼   teaspoon salt
¼   teaspoon freshly ground black pepper

1. Preheat oven to 400°. **2. Place** 1 cup broth in a medium saucepan. Cover pan and bring to a boil. Gradually stir in uncooked couscous. Remove from heat; cover and let stand 5 minutes. Fluff couscous with a fork. **3. Heat** a large nonstick skillet over medium-high heat. Coat pan heavily with cooking spray. Add squash and garlic; sauté 2 minutes. Add onions, basil, and oregano; sauté 2 minutes or until squash is tender. Remove from heat. **4. Combine** cheeses in a small bowl. Add couscous and half of cheese mixture to squash mixture; stir in remaining chicken broth, egg substitute, salt, and pepper. Spoon mixture into an 8–inch square glass or ceramic baking dish lightly coated with cooking spray. Top with remaining half of cheese mixture. **5. Bake** at 400° for 30 minutes or until golden. Serve warm. **Yield:** 8 servings (serving size: about ½ cup).

CALORIES 114; FAT 1.9g (sat 0.9g, mono 0.4g, poly 0.3g); PROTEIN 5.6g; CARB 18.5g; FIBER 1.6g; CHOL 5mg; IRON 0.6mg; SODIUM 225mg; CALC 51mg

Creamy Two-Cheese Polenta

Tired of rice and pasta? Give this quick, creamy polenta a try for a dish similar to cheese grits. If you are not serving immediately, keep it covered over low heat, and stir occasionally, adding additional water, if necessary, to prevent it from becoming too thick. Serve with pork tenderloin and a simple green salad.

Young Chefs can:

• Help pour milk and water into saucepan
• Measure Parmigiano-Reggiano cheese

Older Chefs can:

• Measure dry polenta
• Stir in cheeses with adult supervision

4   cups 1% low-fat milk
1   cup water
¼   teaspoon salt
¼   teaspoon freshly ground black pepper
1¼   cups instant dry polenta
⅓   cup (2 ounces) light cream cheese
⅓   cup (1.3 ounces) grated Parmigiano-Reggiano cheese

1. Combine first 4 ingredients in a medium saucepan. Bring to a boil over medium-high heat. Reduce heat to medium; gradually add polenta, stirring constantly with a whisk. Cook, stirring constantly, 2 minutes or until thick. Remove from heat; stir in cheeses. Serve immediately. **Yield:** 8 servings (serving size: about 1 cup).

CALORIES 179; FAT 4.7g (sat 2.4g, mono 0.3g, poly 0g); PROTEIN 8.6g; CARB 25.9g; FIBER 1.7g; CHOL 13mg; IRON 2.3mg; SODIUM 403mg; CALC 227mg

Pecan White and Brown Rice Pilaf

Using part instant white rice and part instant brown rice can help make the switch to whole grains easier.

Young Chefs can:

- Add bay leaf to pan with adult supervision
- Add pecans

Older Chefs can:

- Measure rices and bulgur
- Add rices, bulgur, cranberries, and salt with adult supervision

2	teaspoons olive oil
1	cup finely chopped onion
1	bay leaf
1	cup water
1	cup fat-free, lower-sodium chicken broth
½	cup uncooked instant white rice
½	cup uncooked instant brown rice
½	cup uncooked bulgur
1	tablespoon sweetened dried cranberries
½	teaspoon salt
¼	cup chopped pecans, toasted

1. Heat oil in a large saucepan over medium-high heat. Add onion; sauté 4 minutes or until tender. Add bay leaf; cook 1 minute. Add 1 cup water and next 6 ingredients. Bring to a boil; cover, reduce heat, and simmer 8 minutes or until rice is done and liquid is absorbed. Remove from heat. Let stand, covered, 5 minutes. Discard bay leaf; add pecans. Fluff with a fork. **Yield:** 9 servings (serving size: ½ cup).

CALORIES 109; FAT 3.5g (sat 0.4g, mono 2g, poly 0.8g); PROTEIN 2.8g; CARB 17.6g; FIBER 2.3g; CHOL 0mg; IRON 0.7mg; SODIUM 196mg; CALC 9mg

kitchen classroom
New Ideas for Preparing Vegetables

Experimenting with new seasonings and cooking methods can be daunting. Try some of these ideas to dress up ordinary vegetables and make a new delicious side dish using ingredients you probably already have on hand.

Baking or Roasting

Good vegetables to try: Sweet potatoes, potatoes, asparagus, green beans, squash, zucchini, onions, Brussels sprouts

Seasonings: Add salt and pepper to potatoes when done. For other vegetables, toss with olive oil, fresh or dried garlic, salt, and pepper prior to roasting.

How to: Bake directly on rack (for whole potatoes) or on roasting pan or cookie sheet.

Grilling

Good vegetables to try: Zucchini, asparagus, squash, corn on the cob, green beans, portobello or button mushrooms

Seasonings: Toss vegetables in olive oil, minced garlic, salt, and pepper. Add a little balsamic vinegar for added flavor.

How to: Grill directly on rack, on skewers, wrapped in foil, or in a grill sauté basket.

Steaming

Good vegetables to try: Asparagus, broccoli, corn, carrots, green beans, cauliflower

Seasonings: Toss steamed vegetables with olive oil, lemon juice, or a light vinaigrette. Sprinkle with toasted nuts, or mix with sautéed garlic and onions.

How to: Steam with water in basket in saucepan or in microwave. Toss with seasonings.

Snacks

Quick ways to energize bodies for learning and play

Snacks

Kids are very active, so it is essential to fuel their bodies properly. Snacking is a great way to keep energy levels up and minds alert, as well as get in extra nutrients. However, many store-bought snack foods marketed toward kids leave much to be desired nutritionally. This chapter is designed to give parents some quick, healthy alternatives to processed foods and junk foods.

Cinnamon Popcorn

Adding a touch of salt brings out the sweet cinnamon flavor. Store in an airtight container to keep fresh.

Young Chefs can:

- Pour cooled popcorn into large bowl
- Sprinkle cinnamon mixture over popcorn

Older Chefs can:

- Coat popcorn with cooking spray
- Measure and combine sugar, salt, and cinnamon

1	(2.9-ounce) bag butter-flavored 94% fat-free microwave popcorn

Cooking spray

2	tablespoons sugar
1	teaspoon ground cinnamon
1/8	teaspoon salt
1½	tablespoons butter, melted

1. Pop popcorn according to package directions. Place popcorn in a large bowl. Lightly coat popcorn with cooking spray, and toss well; repeat. **2. Combine** sugar, cinnamon, and salt. Drizzle popcorn with butter; toss well. Sprinkle with sugar mixture; toss to coat. Serve immediately. **Yield:** 8 servings (serving size: 1 cup).

CALORIES 63; FAT 2.9g (sat 1.4g, mono 0.6g, poly 0.1g); PROTEIN 1.1g; CARB 10.4g; FIBER 1.8g; CHOL 6mg; IRON 0mg; SODIUM 149mg; CALC 4mg

nutrition note

Go-To Snacks

Be prepared when hunger strikes with these quick snacks. Each provides a balance of carbohydrate and protein to keep kids content until mealtime.

- Peanut butter or almond butter on whole-wheat toast, crackers, or rice cakes
- Apple slices and a part-skim mozzarella cheese stick
- Hummus with baby carrots and whole-wheat pita wedges
- Turkey and cheese cubes with whole-wheat crackers
- Berries with fat-free Greek yogurt
- Popcorn and fat-free milk

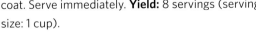

meals made easy =

Cheesy Ranch Popcorn ÷ ÷ strawberries

Cheesy Ranch Popcorn

Most people don't realize that popcorn is a whole grain, which means it's full of fiber. Two quick additions to a low-fat bag of popped corn are all you need to add an extra burst of flavor.

Young Chefs can:

- Pour cooled popcorn into large bowl
- Sprinkle cheese mixture over popcorn

Older Chefs can:

- Coat popcorn with cooking spray
- Measure cheese, and combine cheese-dressing mixture

1   (2.9-ounce) bag butter-flavored 94% fat-free microwave popcorn
Cooking spray
¼   cup grated Parmesan cheese
2   teaspoons dry ranch dressing mix

1. Pop popcorn according to package directions. Place popcorn in a large bowl. Lightly coat popcorn with cooking spray, and toss well; repeat. **2. Combine** cheese and dressing mix; sprinkle over popcorn, tossing well. Serve immediately. **Yield:** 8 servings (serving size: 1 cup).

CALORIES 51; FAT 1.5g (sat 0.7g, mono 0.3g, poly 0.3g); PROTEIN 2g; CARB 7.5g; FIBER 1.3g; CHOL 2mg; IRON 0mg; SODIUM 222mg; CALC 28mg

Fruit Salsa

Baked cinnamon pita chips make the perfect scoop for this naturally sweet fruit mixture. Serve extra salsa as a topping for yogurt or angel food cake.

Young Chefs can:

- Wash strawberries and apple
- Add measured chopped fruit to bowl

Older Chefs can:

- Carefully help dice strawberries with dinner knife
- Squeeze and measure lime juice

1   cup finely diced strawberries
1   cup finely diced unpeeled Granny Smith apple
½   cup finely diced mango
2   tablespoons orange juice
1   tablespoon fresh lime juice
1   teaspoon sugar

1. Combine all ingredients in a medium bowl, tossing to coat. Cover and chill 2 hours. **Yield:** 8 servings (serving size: ¼ cup).

CALORIES 26; FAT 0.1g (sat 0g, mono 0g, poly 0.1g); PROTEIN 0.3g; CARB 6.6g; FIBER 1g; CHOL 0mg; IRON 0.1mg; SODIUM 1mg; CALC 6mg

snacks

Key Lime Dip with Fresh Fruit Kebabs

Cubes of melon or apple chunks make great summer additions to this fun fruit treat.

Young Chefs can:

• Wash grapes and strawberries
• Line up fruit in the order it is to be threaded

Older Chefs can:

• Combine and mix dip ingredients
• Carefully thread fruit on skewers

1½ cups (12 ounces) block-style light cream cheese
3   tablespoons powdered sugar
1   teaspoon grated lime rind
1   (6-ounce) carton key lime pie light yogurt

2   cups strawberries
1   cup seedless red grapes
1   cup pineapple chunks (about 12 chunks)
2   kiwifruit, peeled and cut into wedges
12 (6-inch) wooden skewers

1. Combine first 4 ingredients in a medium bowl; beat with a mixer at medium speed until smooth. Cover and refrigerate while preparing fruit kebabs. **2. Thread** fruit alternately onto each wooden skewer. Serve with dip. **Yield:** 6 servings (serving size: ⅓ cup dip and 2 fruit kebabs).

CALORIES 218; FAT 9.1g (sat 5.9g, mono 0g, poly 0.2g); PROTEIN 7.4g; CARB 28.6g; FIBER 2.3g; CHOL 30mg; IRON 0.5mg; SODIUM 298mg; CALC 244mg

"I love the flavor of the dip! It was great with strawberries."

Hannah, age 11

"It was very creamy and had a lot of flavor.
I want to eat this with cucumbers."

Ella, age 10

Creamy Hummus

The fiber, complex carbs, and protein in the chickpeas combined with heart-healthy olive oil are what make hummus such a perfect snack food. Serve with warm whole-wheat pita bread triangles or cut-up vegetables.

Young Chefs can:

- Pour chickpeas in colander to drain and rinse
- Add measured ingredients to food processor

Older Chefs can:

- Measure tahini and lemon juice
- Drop garlic in food chute with adult supervision

2	peeled garlic cloves
¼	cup tahini (roasted sesame-seed paste)
3	tablespoons fresh lemon juice
2	tablespoons water
1	tablespoon extra-virgin olive oil
½	teaspoon ground cumin
¼	teaspoon salt
1	(19-ounce) can chickpeas (garbanzo beans), rinsed and drained

1. Drop garlic through food chute with processor on; process 15 seconds or until minced. Add tahini and remaining ingredients; process 30 seconds or until smooth, scraping sides occasionally. **Yield:** 8 servings (serving size: about ¼ cup).

CALORIES 113; FAT 6.2g (sat 0.9g, mono 3g, poly 2.1g); PROTEIN 3.5g; CARB 11.8g; FIBER 2.3g; CHOL 0mg; IRON 1mg; SODIUM 151mg; CALC 27mg

Layered Bean Dip

Organic refried beans often have half the sodium of conventional beans but can have a drier texture. We added a little lime juice to smooth out the beans and enhance the flavor. Serve with store-bought baked tortilla chips or Baked Whole-Wheat Tortilla Chips (page 113).

Young Chefs can:

- Help spread salsa over beans
- Sprinkle cheese over corn mixture

Older Chefs can:

- Spread bean mixture in baking dish
- Stir together corn, green onions, and olives

2	teaspoons fresh lime juice
½	teaspoon ground cumin
1	(16-ounce) can organic refried beans
Cooking spray	
1	cup organic bottled salsa
⅔	cup frozen whole-kernel corn, thawed
¼	cup chopped green onions
2	tablespoons chopped black olives
¾	cup (3 ounces) preshredded reduced-fat 4-cheese Mexican blend cheese
¾	cup light sour cream
2	tablespoons chopped fresh cilantro

1. Preheat oven to 350°. **2. Combine** first 3 ingredients in a medium bowl. Spread bean mixture evenly into an 11 x 7-inch glass or ceramic baking dish coated with cooking spray. Spread salsa evenly over beans. **3. Combine** corn, green onions, and olives; spoon corn mixture evenly over salsa. Sprinkle cheese over corn mixture. **4. Bake,** uncovered, at 350° for 20 minutes or until bubbly. Let stand 10 minutes. Top with sour cream; sprinkle with cilantro. **Yield:** 12 servings (serving size: ½ cup).

CALORIES 102; FAT 4.1g (sat 1.5g, mono 0.5g, poly 0.1g); PROTEIN 5.2g; CARB 12g; FIBER 2.1g; CHOL 10mg; IRON 0.7mg; SODIUM 325mg; CALC 78mg

"It has lots of healthy green stuff, and I like it. I would eat this with carrots."

Adeline, age 5

Spinach-Parmesan Dip

The spinach may seem like it will overflow in the skillet, but keep stirring—as it begins to wilt, it reduces in volume. Serve this creamy dip with baby carrots, cucumber slices, or whole-grain pita chips.

Young Chefs can:

- Tear spinach leaves
- Push buttons on food processor with adult supervision

Older Chefs can:

- Measure yogurt and cheese
- Stir yogurt and cheese into spinach mixture

1	teaspoon olive oil
2	garlic cloves, minced
1	(9-ounce) package fresh spinach
¼	teaspoon salt
½	cup fresh basil leaves, loosely packed
⅓	cup (about 3 ounces) ⅓-less-fat cream cheese, softened
⅓	cup plain fat-free yogurt
¼	cup (1 ounce) grated fresh Parmesan cheese

1. **Heat** olive oil in a large skillet over medium-high heat. Add garlic; sauté 1 minute. Add spinach and salt; sauté 2 minutes or until spinach wilts. Place spinach mixture in a colander, pressing until mixture is barely moist. 2. **Place** spinach mixture, basil, and cream cheese in a food processor; process until smooth. Spoon spinach mixture into a medium bowl. Stir in yogurt and Parmesan cheese. Cover and chill. **Yield:** 6 servings (serving size: ¼ cup).

CALORIES 87; FAT 5.2g (sat 2.8g, mono 0.6g, poly 0.1g); PROTEIN 5.3g; CARB 6.5g; FIBER 2.1g; CHOL 14mg; IRON 1.5mg; SODIUM 319mg; CALC 132mg

Limiting Trans Fats

The snack aisle is full of kid-friendly snack foods, but parents beware! Not only do many of these foods have added sugars, but many also contain a harmful type of fat known as trans fat, which has been shown to increase LDL ("bad" cholesterol) levels and raise heart disease risk. Trans fats are predominantly found in products that contain partially hydrogenated vegetable oil, a fat often used in processed foods like cookies, crackers, peanut butter, and other snack foods to make them more shelf-stable and stay fresh-tasting longer.

So what's a parent to do? The FDA now requires that food labels list trans fat amounts. However, products may still contain some trans fats if the amount on the label is less than 0.5 grams of trans fat *per serving.* So check the ingredient list to be sure you don't see the words "partially hydrogenated" to ensure the product is truly free of trans fats. You can also choose fewer processed foods by shopping the perimeter of the grocery store where healthier items like fruits, veggies, and yogurt are located. Finally, avoid foods known to have a lot of trans fats, such as fried foods, margarines, and shortenings.

Whole-Wheat Garlic Pita Chips

Pita chips are a tasty, nutritious base for dips and spreads such as hummus and salsa. They also make a crisp accompaniment to salads and soups.

Young Chefs can:

- Count out pitas and wedges after they're cut
- Place wedges on baking sheet

Older Chefs can:

- Spray pita wedges with cooking spray
- Sprinkle salt and garlic powder over pita wedges

3 (6-inch) whole-wheat pitas, split horizontally
Olive oil–flavored cooking spray
½ teaspoon kosher salt
¼ teaspoon garlic powder

1. Preheat oven to 350°. **2. Cut** each pita half into 8 wedges, creating 48 wedges. Arrange wedges in single layers on 2 baking sheets. Coat wedges with cooking spray; sprinkle evenly with salt and garlic powder. **3. Bake** at 350° for 12 to 14 minutes or until toasted. Cool. Store in an airtight container. **Yield:** 6 servings (serving size: 8 chips).

CALORIES 87; FAT 1g (sat 0.1g, mono 0.1g, poly 0.3g); PROTEIN 3.2g; CARB 17.7g; FIBER 2.4g; CHOL 0mg; IRON 1mg; SODIUM 330mg; CALC 5mg

Baked Whole-Wheat Tortilla Chips

Making your own tortilla chips allows you to add whole grains and keep fat grams down. Serve with your favorite salsa or dip.

Young Chefs can:

- Arrange wedges on baking sheets
- Sprinkle salt on wedges

Older Chefs can:

- Cut tortillas into wedges with safety scissors or adult supervision
- Coat wedges with cooking spray

6   (8-inch) whole-wheat or whole-grain flour tortillas
Cooking spray
½   teaspoon kosher salt

1. Preheat oven to 350°. **2. Cut** each tortilla into 8 wedges, creating 48 wedges. Arrange wedges in single layers on 2 baking sheets. Lightly coat wedges with cooking spray; sprinkle evenly with salt. **3. Bake** at 350° for 15 minutes or until lightly browned and crisp. Cool. Store in an airtight container. **Yield:** 6 servings (serving size: 8 chips).

CALORIES 98; FAT 0.9g (sat 0g, mono 0g, poly 0g); PROTEIN 3.2g; CARB 18.4g; FIBER 0.8g; CHOL 0mg; IRON 0.6mg; SODIUM 320mg; CALC 48mg

Quick Snack Mix

Combining these favorite snacks gives a fresh spin to each and offers a wider variety of nutrients. Feel free to substitute other similar snack items you may have on hand.

Young Chefs can:

- Pour cooled popcorn into bowl
- Add all measured ingredients to bowl

Older Chefs can:

- Pick out unpopped kernels from popcorn
- Measure and combine ingredients

1   (1.2-ounce) bag 94% fat-free microwave popcorn, popped
2   cups cinnamon-sugar whole-wheat and rice cereal
1   cup tiny hard pretzel twists, salted
1   cup honey-flavored bear-shaped graham crackers
1   cup whole-grain fish-shaped cheese crackers
½   cup raisins
½   cup candy-coated milk chocolate pieces

1. Remove unpopped kernels from popcorn, and discard kernels. Combine all ingredients in a large bowl. Store in an airtight container. **Yield:** 9 servings (serving size: about 1 cup).

CALORIES 195; FAT 5.1g (sat 1.8g, mono 1.2g, poly 1g); PROTEIN 3.6g; CARB 36.4g; FIBER 2.8g; CHOL 2mg; IRON 3.1mg; SODIUM 255mg; CALC 196mg

"I like the crunchy and sweet. This snack mix would be good in my school lunch."

Nathan, age 6

Snacking Smart

Snacking is a completely normal—and healthy—way for kids to get needed energy and nutrients between meals, as long as good food choices are made. Here are a few tips to help both kids and adults snack smart.

Plan Ahead. Having your kitchen full of nutritious food choices will make putting together a healthy snack much easier. Stock your refrigerator with cut-up fruit and vegetables, fat-free yogurt or cottage cheese, part-skim cheese sticks, lean deli meat, and hummus. Good pantry staples to have on hand are popcorn, whole-grain crackers, whole-grain cereals with little added sugar (see "How To Pick a Healthy Breakfast Cereal" on page 31), unsweetened applesauce, natural peanut butter, and rice cakes.

Set Guidelines. Establish regular snack times, and try to stick to those. Smaller kids usually need both a mid-morning and mid-afternoon snack, while older children may need just one. Also, have kids sit at the dinner table or kitchen counter and stop their other activities while eating. Snacks should be viewed as smaller regular meals.

Mix and Match. To keep energy levels up, try pairing a carbohydrate food with a low-fat protein food at each snack (see page 106 for ideas). Carbohydrates fuel kids for activities while protein provides satiety. Avoid foods with added sugars such as sodas, candy, and sweet snack foods, which can cause dips in blood sugar levels and make energy levels (and moods) sag shortly after eating.

Apricot-Almond Gorp

Gorp is another name for trail mix and makes a great portable snack with lots of fiber. Pack in an individual reusable container, and stash in a purse, backpack, or diaper bag for hunger "emergencies."

Young Chefs can:

- Measure nuts and dried fruit
- Combine measured oats and nuts

Older Chefs can:

- Measure oats and honey
- Stir dried fruit into oat mixture

Cooking spray
2¾ cups old-fashioned rolled oats
½ cup slivered almonds
⅓ cup coarsely chopped walnuts
½ cup honey
⅓ cup butter
½ cup dried cherries
½ cup coarsely chopped dried apricots
⅓ cup golden raisins

1. Preheat oven to 350°. **2. Line** a jelly-roll pan with foil; coat foil with cooking spray. Combine oats, almonds, and walnuts in a medium bowl. Place honey and butter in a small saucepan. Cook over low heat 3 minutes or until blended and smooth, stirring occasionally. Drizzle honey mixture over oat mixture; toss to coat. Spread mixture in prepared pan. **3. Bake** at 350° for 15 minutes; stir. Bake an additional 10 minutes or until lightly browned. Cool completely in pan on a wire rack. Stir in cherries, apricots, and raisins.
Yield: 12 servings (serving size: ½ cup).

CALORIES 262; FAT 10.9g (sat 3.8g, mono 3.5g, poly 2.7g); PROTEIN 4.3g; CARB 38.8g; FIBER 3.9g; CHOL 14mg; IRON 1.7mg; SODIUM 39mg; CALC 30mg

Chocolate-Cranberry Crunch

This trail mix makes a large quantity, but it can be stored in an airtight container for up to a week. It's delicious as a topping for low-fat yogurt or ice cream.

Young Chefs can:

• Pour measured oats, cereal, and nuts into bowl
• Measure dried cranberries

Older Chefs can:

• Measure oats, cereal, brown sugar, and pecans
• Spread chocolate-oat mixture onto pan

Cooking spray
3   cups old-fashioned rolled oats
1   cup crispy wheat cereal squares
½   cup packed light brown sugar
⅓   cup chopped pecans
½   teaspoon salt
¼   teaspoon ground cinnamon
¼   cup honey
2   tablespoons canola oil
1   teaspoon vanilla extract
2   ounces semisweet chocolate, finely chopped
½   cup sweetened dried cranberries

1. Preheat oven to 300°. **2. Line** a jelly-roll pan with parchment paper. Coat parchment with cooking spray. **3. Combine** oats and next 5 ingredients in a large bowl. Combine honey and canola oil in a small saucepan. Cook over low heat 2 minutes or until warm. Remove from heat. Add vanilla and chocolate, stirring with a whisk until smooth. Gently stir chocolate mixture into oat mixture. **4. Spread** chocolate mixture onto prepared pan. Bake at 300° for 28 minutes, stirring twice. Cool completely in pan on a wire rack. Stir in cranberries. Store in an airtight container for up to 1 week. **Yield:** 12 servings (serving size: ½ cup).

CALORIES 232; FAT 7.6g (sat 1.5g, mono 3.2g, poly 1.9g); PROTEIN 3.7g; CARB 40.2g; FIBER 3.4g; CHOL 0mg; IRON 2.6mg; SODIUM 144mg; CALC 22mg

Honey-Glazed Nuts

Nuts and seeds are a good source of healthy fats and protein that pack well for the road. Use any variety of mixed nuts or seeds.

Young Chefs can:

- Measure chopped nuts
- Measure sunflower seeds

Older Chefs can:

- Measure spices
- Help add nuts, seeds, and spices to skillet with adult supervision

Cooking spray
1   teaspoon butter
¼   cup honey
¼   cup slivered almonds
¼   cup chopped hazelnuts
¼   cup chopped pecans
¼   cup sunflower seeds
½   teaspoon ground cinnamon
¼   teaspoon ground cardamom
¼   teaspoon salt
⅛   teaspoon ground cloves

1. Line a baking sheet with parchment paper; coat parchment with cooking spray. **2. Heat** butter in a large nonstick skillet over medium-high heat. Stir in honey; cook 2 minutes or until mixture bubbles around edges of pan. Add almonds and remaining ingredients, and cook over medium heat 4 to 5 minutes or until nuts are golden, stirring frequently. Immediately spread onto prepared baking sheet; cool completely. **Yield:** 6 servings (serving size: ¼ cup).

CALORIES 166; FAT 11.7g (sat 1.3g, mono 5.6g, poly 1.9g); PROTEIN 3.3g; CARB 15.2g; FIBER 2.1g; CHOL 2mg; IRON 0.9mg; SODIUM 102mg; CALC 31mg

Peanut Butter–Banana Waffles

No knife and fork needed—just use your hands like you would when eating an open-faced sandwich.

Young Chefs can:

- Break mini waffles apart
- Top waffles with banana slices

Older Chefs can:

- Stir together peanut butter and honey
- Slice banana with dinner knife

4   frozen mini waffles
1   tablespoon natural-style peanut butter
2   teaspoons honey
½   small banana, sliced

1. Toast waffles according to package directions.
2. While waffles cook, combine peanut butter and honey. Spread mixture over waffles, and top with banana slices. **Yield:** 2 servings (serving size: 2 topped mini waffles).

CALORIES 129; FAT 2.6g (sat 0.5g, mono 0g, poly 0g); PROTEIN 2.8g; CARB 19.3g; FIBER 1.3g; CHOL 0mg; IRON 0.5mg; SODIUM 121mg; CALC 52mg

nutrition note
Peanut Butter Tip

Natural peanut butter lacks the added sugar and hydrogenated fats that other peanut butters have, making it a healthier option. The downside, though, is that spreading it can be hard after it is stored in the refrigerator. To make spreading easier, microwave it a few seconds to soften, and then stir well.

"I liked it because I like banana bread, and this tastes like good banana bread with lots of walnuts."

Parker, age 12

Monkey Bars

Juice rehydrates the raisins so they stay plump while baking. This moist snacking cake might remind you of banana bread.

Young Chefs can:

- Mash banana
- Measure raisins and walnuts

Older Chefs can:

- Stir together dry ingredients
- Stir raisin mixture and walnuts into batter

½ cup raisins
1½ tablespoons apple juice
4.5 ounces all-purpose flour (about 1 cup)
½ teaspoon baking powder
½ teaspoon baking soda
¼ teaspoon salt
¾ cup packed brown sugar
¼ cup butter, softened
½ cup mashed ripe banana (1 medium)
3 tablespoons low-fat buttermilk
1 teaspoon vanilla extract
2 large egg whites
⅓ cup chopped walnuts
Cooking spray
1 tablespoon powdered sugar

1. Preheat oven to 350°. **2. Combine** raisins and apple juice in a microwave-safe bowl. Microwave at HIGH 1 minute. Weigh or lightly spoon flour into a dry measuring cup; level with a knife. Combine flour and next 3 ingredients in a bowl; stir with a whisk. Combine brown sugar and butter in a large bowl, and beat with a mixer at medium speed until blended. Add banana and next 3 ingredients, beating well. Add flour mixture, beating just until combined. Stir in raisin mixture and walnuts. **3. Spread** batter in an 8-inch square metal baking pan coated with cooking spray. Bake at 350° for 30 minutes or until a wooden pick inserted in center comes out clean. Cool completely on a wire rack. Sprinkle with powdered sugar, and cut into bars. **Yield:** 16 servings (serving size: 1 bar).

CALORIES 137; FAT 4.7g (sat 2g, mono 1g, poly 1.3g); PROTEIN 2g; CARB 22.7g; FIBER 0.7g; CHOL 8mg; IRON 0.6mg; SODIUM 122mg; CALC 27mg

kitchen classroom

Ripe Bananas

When selecting bananas, the only way to tell how ripe they are is by the color of the peel. The skin of a perfectly ripe banana will be yellow and slightly speckled with brown spots. It'll be softer and sweeter than green bananas (or even slightly green ones), which are not yet ripe.

Banana Multigrain Bars

Serve these moist cakelike bars as a snack or for breakfast. A multigrain hot cereal is a key ingredient in the batter.

Young Chefs can:

- Mash banana
- Pour flour mixture into banana mixture

Older Chefs can:

- Measure brown sugar, cereal, and pecans
- Stir cereal and pecans into batter

Cooking spray
½ cup mashed ripe banana (1 medium)
⅓ cup packed brown sugar
¼ cup honey
1 tablespoon vegetable oil
½ teaspoon vanilla extract
1 large egg
2.2 ounces all-purpose flour (about ½ cup)
½ teaspoon salt
1¼ cups multigrain hot cereal
¼ cup chopped pecans

1. Preheat oven to 350°. **2. Coat** a foil-lined 8-inch square metal baking pan with cooking spray. **3. Place** banana and next 5 ingredients in a medium bowl; beat with a mixer at medium speed until blended. Weigh or lightly spoon flour into a dry measuring cup; level with a knife. Combine flour and salt in a bowl, stirring with a whisk. Gradually add flour mixture to banana mixture. Stir in cereal and pecans. **4. Spoon** batter into prepared pan. Bake at 350° for 25 minutes. Cool completely on a wire rack. Cut into bars. **Yield:** 12 servings (serving size: 1 bar).

CALORIES 132; FAT 3.6g (sat 0.5g, mono 1.6g, poly 1.2g); PROTEIN 2.3g; CARB 24.4g; FIBER 1.6g; CHOL 18mg; IRON 0.7mg; SODIUM 105mg; CALC 13mg

Chewy Coconut-Granola Bars

Store-bought granola bars too often resemble candy bars with swirls of peanut butter and caramel drizzles, so make one from scratch that features whole-wheat flour, whole-grain granola, and fruit.

Young Chefs can:

- Pour measured granola and fruit into batter
- Sprinkle coconut over batter

Older Chefs can:

- Stir together flours
- Measure brown sugar, granola, and coconut

Cooking spray
2   teaspoons all-purpose flour
3   ounces all-purpose flour (about ⅔ cup)
1.6 ounces whole-wheat flour (about ⅓ cup)
1   teaspoon baking powder
½   teaspoon salt
1¼   cups packed brown sugar
¼   cup vegetable oil
2   tablespoons fat-free milk
2   large eggs
1½   cups whole-grain granola
¾   cup chopped dried mixed tropical fruit
½   cup flaked sweetened coconut

1. Preheat oven to 350°. **2. Coat** a 13 x 9–inch metal baking pan with cooking spray; dust with 2 teaspoons all-purpose flour. **3. Weigh** or lightly spoon 3 ounces all-purpose flour and 1.6 ounces whole-wheat flour into dry measuring cups; level with a knife. Combine flours, baking powder, and salt in a small bowl; stir with a whisk. Combine sugar and next 3 ingredients in a large bowl; beat with a mixer at high speed until smooth. Add flour mixture, beating at low speed until blended. Fold in granola and fruit. Spoon batter into prepared pan. Sprinkle with coconut. **4. Bake** at 350° for 20 minutes or until golden. Cool completely in pan on a wire rack. Cut into bars. Store in an airtight container up to 2 weeks. **Yield:** 16 servings (serving size: 1 bar).

CALORIES 153; FAT 5.8g (sat 1.6g, mono 1.8g, poly 1.6g); PROTEIN 2.7g; CARB 23.4g; FIBER 1.7g; CHOL 26mg; IRON 1mg; SODIUM 148mg; CALC 36mg

kitchen classroom

Following Directions and Understanding Order

Following directions is essential when cooking from recipes, but it's something parents sometimes grow weary of reinforcing. Show kids the positive end product of following directions by cooking with them. The actual preparation of a recipe also helps kids see and understand order and why certain steps must be carried out first.

Preschoolers: Let them assist by following your directions ("pour the popcorn in the bowl"). Emphasize words like "first," "next," and "then" to establish order for them.

Younger elementary: Help them read and think through the recipe, and then challenge their listening and memory skills by asking them what they should do first. If they start to make a wrong move, stop them and challenge them to think what might go wrong if they did that certain task in this order.

Older elementary: Let them read the recipe, think through the steps, and then organize and prep their ingredients and utensils. Allow them to complete the recipe from start to finish (unless adult assistance is needed).

Desserts

Sweet treats for special occasions

Desserts

We believe that every now and then kids—and adults—deserve a sweet treat. Because most desserts feature sugar and added fat, research has shown that teaching moderation—incorporating sweets occasionally and in appropriate amounts rather than completely eliminating them—will actually help your child develop healthier eating habits down the road. This chapter features recipes kids will love that are moderate in both fat and sugar.

Arctic Lime Freeze

You're probably thinking there's no way a dessert with tofu in it could ever be good, right? Well, think again because silken tofu can give a creamy, rich texture to smoothies and frozen desserts like this one. Tofu is also a great source of protein, B vitamins, calcium, and iron—all nutrients that kids need.

Young Chefs can:

- Stack paper towels to drain tofu
- Put top on blender, and press blender buttons with adult supervision

Older Chefs can:

- Add limeade and tofu to blender, and blend ingredients with adult supervision
- Pour mixture into ice-cream freezer

1   (12-ounce) can thawed limeade concentrate, undiluted
1   (12.3-ounce) package light silken firm tofu, drained
1½ cups water

1. Place concentrate and tofu in a blender; process until smooth. Pour mixture into the freezer can of an ice-cream freezer; stir in 1½ cups water. Freeze according to manufacturer's instructions. Spoon mixture into a freezer-safe container; cover and freeze 2 hours or until firm. **Yield:** 10 servings (serving size: ½ cup).

CALORIES 97; FAT 0.2g (sat 0.1g, mono 0.1g, poly 0.1g); PROTEIN 2.1g; CARB 21.6g; FIBER 0g; CHOL 0mg; IRON 0.3mg; SODIUM 29mg; CALC 9mg

Peppermint Ice Cream

Crushed peppermint candies turn this ice cream light pink. This is a great make-ahead recipe; if it's frozen solid, remove it from the freezer before serving so it can soften.

Young Chefs can:

- Count out candies
- Add crushed candies

Older Chefs can:

- Unwrap candies, and measure crushed candies
- Pour mixture into ice-cream freezer

2½ cups 2% reduced-fat milk, divided
2 large egg yolks
2 teaspoons vanilla extract
1 (14-ounce) can fat-free sweetened condensed milk
2/3 cup crushed peppermint candies (about 26 candies)

1. **Combine** 1¼ cups reduced-fat milk and egg yolks in a heavy saucepan over medium heat, stirring with a whisk. Cook over medium heat 9 minutes or until mixture is slightly thick and coats the back of a spoon, stirring constantly (do not boil). Cool egg mixture slightly.
2. **Combine** remaining 1¼ cups reduced-fat milk, vanilla, and condensed milk in a large bowl. Gradually add egg mixture, stirring with a whisk. Cover and chill thoroughly. Stir in crushed candies. Pour mixture into the freezer can of an ice-cream freezer; freeze according to manufacturer's instructions. Spoon ice cream into a freezer-safe container; cover and freeze 1 hour or until firm. **Yield:** 8 servings (serving size: ½ cup).

CALORIES 227; FAT 2.6g (sat 1.4g, mono 0.9g, poly 0.2g); PROTEIN 7g; CARB 40.9g; FIBER 0g; CHOL 65mg; IRON 0.1mg; SODIUM 84mg; CALC 222mg

Peach Ice Cream

Ripe peaches at peak season are key to this creamy, refreshing ice cream. Take your kids to a local peach orchard or farmers' market and let them hand-pick the peaches.

Young Chefs can:

- Put top on blender, and press blender buttons with adult supervision
- Add measured sugar to peaches

Older Chefs can:

- Place peaches in blender, and blend peaches with adult supervision
- Pour mixture into ice-cream freezer

3 cups sliced peeled peaches (about 1½ pounds)
1 cup half-and-half
½ cup sugar
½ cup whole milk
1 teaspoon vanilla extract

1. **Place** peaches in a blender or food processor; process until finely chopped. Combine peaches, half-and-half, and remaining ingredients in a large bowl. Pour peach mixture into the freezer can of an ice-cream freezer; freeze according to manufacturer's instructions. Spoon ice cream into a freezer-safe container; cover and freeze 2 hours or until firm. **Yield:** 8 servings (serving size: ½ cup).

CALORIES 121; FAT 4.1g (sat 2.4g, mono 1.2g, poly 0.2g); PROTEIN 1.9g; CARB 20.2g; FIBER 0.8g; CHOL 13mg; IRON 0.2mg; SODIUM 18mg; CALC 52mg

Sweets: A Sticky Parenting Dilemma

Lollipops at the doctor's office, birthday cakes at parties, cookies at grandma's house—does it seem that sugary treats are constantly offered to your kids? The rise of childhood obesity is a cause of concern for parents and health professionals. The solution is not to totally eliminate sweets but rather to help your child find a balance between a little and too much indulgence. Teaching moderation can be a difficult parenting task, but these guidelines will help make it a little less sticky.

Let them eat cake. On occasion, that is. Forbidding any food makes a person want it that much more. Allow your child to have dessert, but don't serve it every night. Let it mark a special occasion such as the end of the school week or a birthday.

Rethink dessert. All desserts don't have to be as decadent as an ice-cream sundae. Expand your definition of dessert by offering fruit and dairy-based options such as all-fruit popsicles, fruit-flavored gelatin, fat-free pudding, and smoothies.

Suggest new ideas. School parties often serve more cupcakes and candy than any child could ever wish for. Talk to your child's teacher and suggest paring back the sugary foods or replacing them with popcorn, juice, and games.

Teach by example. Kids need to see parents eating nutritious foods daily, as well as indulging in treats on occasion. Explain to kids that there are healthy foods we need every day and less healthy foods that we don't need as much.

Raspberry Frozen Yogurt

Yogurt and milk add calcium and make this icy dessert extra creamy.

Young Chefs can:

- Pour yogurt into bowl
- Place top on blender, and press blender buttons with adult supervision

Older Chefs can:

- Stir yogurt-milk mixture
- Strain raspberry puree

2   cups French vanilla low-fat yogurt
½   cup whole milk
¼   cup sugar
1   (10-ounce) package frozen raspberries
        in syrup, thawed
Fresh raspberries (optional)

1. Combine first 3 ingredients in a large bowl, stirring until sugar dissolves. **2. Place** thawed raspberries in a blender; process until smooth. Strain puree through a fine sieve over a bowl. Discard seeds. Stir puree into yogurt mixture. **3. Pour** raspberry mixture into the freezer can of an ice-cream freezer; freeze according to manufacturer's instructions. Spoon yogurt mixture into a freezer-safe container; cover and freeze 1 hour or until firm. Scoop into small dessert dishes, and garnish with fresh raspberries, if desired. **Yield:** 8 servings (serving size: about ½ cup).

CALORIES 100; FAT 1.3g (sat 0.8g, mono 0.3g, poly 0.1g); PROTEIN 3.8g; CARB 18.6g; FIBER 0.5g; CHOL 5mg; IRON 0.2mg; SODIUM 47mg; CALC 124mg

Summer Berry Popsicles

The key to these homemade pops is choosing super-sweet, ripe fruit. You can freeze these popsicles in small paper cups. Just cover cups with foil, and insert wooden sticks through foil. The foil will hold the sticks upright while the popsicles freeze. Peaches make a good substitute for the berries.

Young Chefs can:

- Wash strawberries
- Add measured fruit to blender

Older Chefs can:

- Hull strawberries with adult supervision
- Press mixture through a sieve

1	cup strawberries, hulled
¾	cup blueberries
¾	cup raspberries
1	small ripe banana
2	tablespoons lemon juice
2	cups vanilla fat-free yogurt
¼	cup sugar

1. Place first 5 ingredients in a blender; process until smooth. Press mixture through a sieve over a bowl; discard solids. Return fruit mixture to blender. Add yogurt and sugar; process until smooth. **2. Pour** yogurt mixture into 2.5-ounce popsicle molds according to manufacturer's instructions. Freeze 3 hours. **Yield:** 12 servings (serving size: 1 popsicle).

CALORIES 79; FAT 0.5g (sat 0.3g, mono 0g, poly 0.1g); PROTEIN 1.7g; CARB 17.9g; FIBER 1.3g; CHOL 3mg; IRON 0.2mg; SODIUM 25mg; CALC 55mg

"The flavor was so fruity and very good."

Mary Douglas, age 9

Chocolate Turtle Brownie Sundaes

Moms will love the convenience that brownie mix and caramel topping give to this semi-homemade dessert. These sundaes are best when the brownies are still slightly warm. We suggest serving in bowls to catch every bite and prevent runny messes.

Young Chefs can:

- Add brownie mix to bowl
- Place cooked brownie in each sundae dish

Older Chefs can:

- Spoon batter into baking dish
- Assemble sundaes

½ (20.5-ounce) package low-fat fudge brownie mix (about 2 cups)

¼ cup water

1 large egg white

Cooking spray

⅓ cup fat-free caramel topping

3 tablespoons chopped pecans, toasted

3 cups vanilla light ice cream, divided

1. Preheat oven to 350°. **2. Combine** 2 cups brownie mix, ¼ cup water, and egg white in a large bowl; stir well with a whisk. Spread batter into an 8-inch square metal baking pan coated with cooking spray. Bake at 350° for 20 minutes. Cool in pan on a wire rack. Cut evenly into 9 servings. **3. Place** caramel topping in a small microwave-safe bowl. Microwave at HIGH 30 seconds, stirring after 15 seconds. Cool slightly. Stir in pecans. **4. Top** each brownie with ⅓ cup ice cream and about 1 tablespoon caramel-pecan topping. **Yield:** 9 servings (serving size: 1 brownie, ⅓ cup ice cream, and about 1 tablespoon sauce).

CALORIES 270; FAT 6.2g (sat 2.1g, mono 1.6g, poly 0.6g); PROTEIN 4g; CARB 50.6g; FIBER 1.4g; CHOL 14mg; IRON 0.9mg; SODIUM 201mg; CALC 84mg

Cinnamon–Tortilla Crisp Sundae

An entire package of 10 tortillas may be prepared and stored in an airtight container for future use; if using all 10, then triple the amounts of butter, cinnamon, and sugar. The tortilla crisps make a nice accompaniment to yogurt as well.

Young Chefs can:

- Cut tortillas into wedges using safety scissors
- Stick tortilla crisps into sundaes

Older Chefs can:

- Sprinkle tortilla wedges with cinnamon-sugar
- Drizzle caramel topping

2 tablespoons sugar
1½ teaspoons ground cinnamon
3 (8-inch) whole-wheat flour tortillas, each cut into 6 wedges
1 tablespoon butter, melted
⅓ cup fat-free caramel topping
3 cups vanilla light ice cream

1. **Preheat** oven to 450°. 2. **Combine** sugar and cinnamon. Arrange tortilla wedges on a baking sheet. Brush both sides of tortilla wedges with butter; sprinkle both sides with cinnamon-sugar mixture. Bake at 450° for 2 to 3 minutes on each side or until lightly browned. 3. **Place** caramel topping in a small microwave-safe bowl. Microwave at HIGH 45 seconds or until melted. Place ½ cup ice cream into each of 6 bowls. Drizzle about 1 tablespoon caramel topping over ice cream in each bowl. Serve each sundae with 3 tortilla wedges. **Yield:** 6 servings (serving size: 1 sundae).

CALORIES 253; FAT 7.6g (sat 3.4g, mono 1.5g, poly 0.2g); PROTEIN 5.7g; CARB 41.6g; FIBER 2.1g; CHOL 26mg; IRON 0.6mg; SODIUM 249mg; CALC 160mg

Cereal and Toffee Dessert Bars

Imaginations can run wild creating different variations of this dessert. Use any combination of crisp cereals and any flavor of light ice cream your family likes.

Young Chefs can:

- Sprinkle crushed candy into ice cream
- Combine measured cereals

Older Chefs can:

- Press cereal mixture into pan
- Spread ice-cream mixture over cereal mixture

4 (1.4-ounce) bars chocolate-covered English toffee candy bars, crushed
8 cups vanilla light ice cream, softened
4 cups crispy rice cereal squares, coarsely crushed
2 cups whole-grain toasted oat cereal
⅔ cup packed dark brown sugar
⅓ cup slivered almonds, toasted
⅓ cup flaked sweetened coconut, toasted
2 tablespoons butter, melted
Cooking spray

1. **Stir** crushed candy into ice cream in a large bowl. Cover and freeze until ready to use. 2. **Combine** rice cereal squares and next 5 ingredients in a large bowl, stirring until well blended. Press 3½ cups cereal mixture in bottom of a 13 x 9-inch metal baking pan coated with cooking spray. 3. **Spread** softened ice-cream mixture over cereal mixture; top evenly with remaining cereal mixture. Cover and freeze 8 hours or until firm. Let stand 5 minutes before cutting into bars. **Yield:** 20 servings (serving size: 1 bar).

CALORIES 259; FAT 10.8g (sat 5.8g, mono 1g, poly 0.3g); PROTEIN 4.6g; CARB 35.1g; FIBER 0.9g; CHOL 37mg; IRON 3.1mg; SODIUM 157mg; CALC 167mg

desserts

Chocolate Fondue

Serve fresh fruit and cut-up angel food cake as dippers for this thick, puddinglike fondue. If you don't have a fondue pot, warm a small bowl for each person. Spoon fondue into bowls, and serve immediately.

Young Chefs can:

- Help sift powdered sugar
- Add measured sugar to saucepan

Older Chefs can:

- Measure milk, and add to saucepan
- Stir chocolate mixture until smooth

2	cups fat-free milk
½	cup powdered sugar, sifted
2	tablespoons all-purpose flour
2	tablespoons dark corn syrup
2	teaspoons vanilla extract
5	ounces semisweet chocolate (about 1 cup), chopped

1. **Bring** first 5 ingredients to a simmer in a large saucepan over medium heat; cook 5 minutes, stirring constantly. Reduce heat to medium-low; cook 2 minutes or until mixture is smooth, stirring constantly.
2. **Place** chocolate in a medium bowl. Pour milk mixture over chocolate; stir until smooth. Transfer chocolate mixture to a fondue pot. Keep warm over a low flame. **Yield:** 24 servings (serving size: 2 tablespoons).

CALORIES 54; FAT 1.7g (sat 1.1g, mono 0g, poly 0g); PROTEIN 1.2g; CARB 9.1g; FIBER 0.3g; CHOL 0mg; IRON 0mg; SODIUM 11mg; CALC 26mg

kitchen classroom
Cooking Chemistry

I f you aren't a science fan, then you may be shocked to learn that cooking is all about chemistry. When you add different food ingredients together, they react—usually with the help of heat—to create a completely new and unique food. If the ingredient amounts or directions aren't followed exactly, then the end product doesn't turn out quite right.

Chemistry is especially important when preparing baked goods like cookies, cakes, muffins, and breads that rely on many of the same ingredients to create deliciously sweet treats. Here's how:

Flour: Often the main ingredient, flour gives batter or dough structure and volume and helps bind all the ingredients together.

Eggs: Eggs are emulsifiers, which means they help all the ingredients blend together. They also give many baked goods some structure and help them rise. Lemon Angel Food Cupcakes on page 135 is an example of a recipe where egg whites are whipped and then incorporated into the batter to create a light, tender cupcake.

Butter: Butter adds flavor and texture to baked treats by making cookies crisp and cakes tender.

Sugar: Sugar is the main source of sweetness in baked goods. It's also responsible for helping the outside of cakes and muffins turn golden brown.

Baking powder and baking soda: Used together or alone, both of these white powders act as leavening agents, which help a batter rise to create tall cakes and muffins.

"I liked these. I would put ice cream between two cookies and make a sandwich."

Ashley, age 12

Cinnamon-Sugar Cookies

Turbinado sugar is less refined and has larger, coarser granules, which glisten on top of sugar cookies. If you prefer a slightly chewier cookie, reduce baking time to 10 minutes.

Young Chefs can:

- Roll dough balls in cinnamon-sugar, and place on baking sheet
- Help combine dry ingredients for cookie dough

Older Chefs can:

- Shape dough into balls
- Stir together sugar and cinnamon

1 cup granulated sugar
6 tablespoons butter, softened
1 tablespoon light corn syrup
1 teaspoon vanilla extract
1 large egg
4 ounces cake flour (about 1 cup)
3.4 ounces all-purpose flour (about ¾ cup)
1 teaspoon baking powder
1 teaspoon baking soda
¼ teaspoon salt
¾ teaspoon ground cinnamon, divided
¼ cup turbinado sugar

1. Place granulated sugar and butter in a bowl; beat with a mixer at medium speed until well blended (about 3 minutes). Add corn syrup, vanilla, and egg; beat 3 minutes or until well blended. **2. Weigh** or lightly spoon flours into dry measuring cups; level with a knife. Combine flours, baking powder, baking soda, salt, and ¼ teaspoon cinnamon. Add flour mixture to butter mixture; stir just until combined. Wrap in plastic wrap; chill 1 hour. **3. Preheat** oven to 375°. **4. Combine** turbinado sugar and remaining ½ teaspoon cinnamon in a small bowl. Shape dough into 56 balls, using about 1 teaspoon of dough each. Roll balls in cinnamon-sugar mixture. Place 2 inches apart on ungreased baking sheets. **5. Bake** at 375° for 10 to 12 minutes or until golden on bottom. Cool on wire racks. **Yield:** 56 servings (serving size: 1 cookie).

CALORIES 43; FAT 1.4g (sat 0.8g, mono 0.4g, poly 0.1g); PROTEIN 0.5g; CARB 7.5g; FIBER 0.1g; CHOL 7mg; IRON 0.3mg; SODIUM 50mg; CALC 6mg

Peanut Butter Jammies

Parents or older kids can beat the cookie dough ingredients with a mixer and let younger kids shape the dough. Just be ready for hand washing afterward since peanut butter is the main ingredient. Use a small spoon to fill the thumbprints with jam.

Young Chefs can:

- Place dough balls on cookie sheet
- Indent cookies with thumb

Older Chefs can:

- Beat ingredients with a mixer with adult supervision
- Roll dough into balls, and spoon jam into indentation

1.5 ounces all-purpose flour (about ⅓ cup)
¾ cup sugar
¾ cup creamy peanut butter
1 large egg, lightly beaten
Cooking spray
¼ cup strawberry jam

1. Preheat oven to 375°. **2. Weigh** or lightly spoon flour into a dry measuring cup; level with a knife. Place sugar, peanut butter, and egg in a medium bowl; beat with a mixer at medium speed until smooth. Add flour; stir well. Shape dough into 30 (1-inch) balls; place 1 inch apart on baking sheets coated with cooking spray. Carefully press thumb into center of each cookie, leaving a slight indentation. **3. Bake** cookies at 375° for 12 minutes or until golden. Remove from pans; cool on wire racks. Spoon ½ teaspoon jam into the center of each cookie. **Yield:** 30 cookies (serving size: 1 cookie).

CALORIES 72; FAT 3.4g (sat 0.7g, mono 1.6g, poly 0.9g); PROTEIN 2g; CARB 9.1g; FIBER 0.4g; CHOL 7mg; IRON 0.2mg; SODIUM 32mg; CALC 4mg

Butterscotch Bars

You'll need about 7 graham cracker sheets to get 1 cup of crumbs.

Young Chefs can:

- Crush graham crackers in a sealed plastic bag
- Measure butterscotch morsels

Older Chefs can:

- Stir together dry ingredients
- Press batter into baking pan

2.25 ounces all-purpose flour (about ½ cup)
1   cup graham cracker crumbs
⅔   cup packed brown sugar
⅓   cup quick-cooking oats
⅓   cup butterscotch morsels
1   teaspoon baking powder
1   tablespoon vegetable oil
1½   teaspoons vanilla extract
2   large egg whites
Cooking spray
1   tablespoon powdered sugar

1. Preheat oven to 350°. **2. Weigh** or lightly spoon flour into a dry measuring cup; level with a knife. Combine flour and next 5 ingredients in a large bowl; stir with a whisk. Combine oil, vanilla, and egg whites in a small bowl, stirring with a whisk; add to flour mixture, stirring just until moist. Lightly coat hands with cooking spray. Press batter into an 8–inch square metal baking pan coated with cooking spray. **3. Bake** at 350° for 18 minutes or until a wooden pick inserted in center comes out clean. Cool in pan on a wire rack. Sift powdered sugar over top. Cut into bars. **Yield:** 12 servings (serving size: 1 bar).

CALORIES 158; FAT 4g (sat 1.8g, mono 0.8g, poly 0.8g); PROTEIN 2g; CARB 28g; FIBER 0.6g; CHOL 0mg; IRON 0.8mg; SODIUM 95mg; CALC 35mg

Ooey-Gooey Peanut Butter–Chocolate Brownies

Make sure to put on aprons before making these.

Young Chefs can:

- Measure peanut butter morsels
- Help press dough into pan

Older Chefs can:

- Spread marshmallow mixture over brownie layer
- Drop remaining dough on marshmallow mixture

¾   cup fat-free sweetened condensed milk, divided
¼   cup butter, melted and cooled
¼   cup fat-free milk
1   (18.25-ounce) package devil's food cake mix
1   large egg white, lightly beaten
Cooking spray
1   (7-ounce) jar marshmallow creme (about 1¾ cups)
½   cup peanut butter morsels

1. Preheat oven to 350°. **2. Combine** ¼ cup condensed milk, butter, and next 3 ingredients in a large bowl (batter will be very stiff). Coat bottom of a 13 x 9–inch metal baking pan with cooking spray. Press two-thirds of dough into prepared pan using fingers coated with cooking spray; pat evenly (layer will be thin). **3. Bake** at 350° for 10 minutes. Combine remaining ½ cup condensed milk and marshmallow creme in a bowl; stir in morsels. Spread marshmallow mixture evenly over brownie layer. Carefully drop remaining dough by spoonfuls over marshmallow mixture. Bake at 350° for 25 minutes (a wooden pick will not test clean). Cool completely in pan on a wire rack. **Yield:** 20 servings (serving size: 1 brownie).

CALORIES 229; FAT 7.2g (sat 4.2g, mono 0.6g, poly 0.1g); PROTEIN 4g; CARB 36.8g; FIBER 0.5g; CHOL 24mg; IRON 1mg; SODIUM 276mg; CALC 56mg

desserts

Cherry-Oatmeal Bars

Young Chefs can:

- Add cherries to filling
- Sprinkle reserved oat mixture over filling

Older Chefs can:

- Press oat mixture into bottom of baking dish
- Spread cherry mixture over oat mixture

4.5 ounces all-purpose flour (about 1 cup)
1   cup quick-cooking oats
½   cup packed brown sugar
¼   teaspoon salt
¼   teaspoon baking soda
¼   teaspoon ground cinnamon
6   tablespoons butter, melted
3   tablespoons orange juice
Cooking spray
½   cup granulated sugar
2   tablespoons all-purpose flour
1   large egg white
1   (8-ounce) container sour cream
1   teaspoon vanilla extract
½   teaspoon grated lemon rind
1   (5-ounce) package dried cherries

1. Preheat oven to 325°. **2. Weigh** or lightly spoon 4.5 ounces flour (about 1 cup) into a dry measuring cup; level with a knife. Combine flour and next 5 ingredients in a medium bowl, stirring with a whisk. Drizzle butter and juice over flour mixture, stirring with a fork until moist (mixture will be crumbly). Reserve ½ cup oat mixture. Press remaining oat mixture into bottom of an 11 x 7-inch glass or ceramic baking dish coated with cooking spray. **3. Combine** granulated sugar and 2 tablespoons flour in a medium bowl, stirring with a whisk. Add egg white and next 3 ingredients, stirring with a whisk until blended. Stir in cherries. Spread cherry mixture over prepared crust; sprinkle reserved oat mixture evenly over filling. **4. Bake** at 325° for 40 minutes or until edges are golden. Cool completely in pan on a wire rack. Cut into bars. **Yield:** 24 servings (serving size: 1 bar).

CALORIES 137; FAT 5.1g (sat 2.9g, mono 1.2g, poly 0.2g); PROTEIN 1.9g; CARB 20.8g; FIBER 1.1g; CHOL 13mg; IRON 0.6mg; SODIUM 70mg; CALC 23mg

Frosted Pumpkin Cake

Pumpkin is full of beta-carotene, a form of vitamin A that keeps eyes healthy and acts as an antioxidant. One serving of this moist cake actually provides more than half of your daily vitamin A needs thanks to the canned pumpkin.

Young Chefs can:

- Add measured flour and sugar to batter
- Help sift powdered sugar

Older Chefs can:

- Beat frosting ingredients with a mixer with adult supervision
- Spread frosting on top of cooled cake

CAKE:

10.1 ounces all-purpose flour (about 2¼ cups)
2½ teaspoons baking powder
2 teaspoons ground cinnamon
¼ teaspoon salt
1 cup packed brown sugar
¼ cup butter, softened
1 teaspoon vanilla extract
2 large eggs
1 (15-ounce) can pumpkin
Cooking spray

FROSTING:

2 tablespoons butter, softened
½ teaspoon vanilla extract
1 (8-ounce) package ⅓-less-fat cream cheese
2 cups sifted powdered sugar

1. Preheat oven to 350°. **2. To prepare cake,** weigh or lightly spoon flour into dry measuring cups; level with a knife. Combine flour and next 3 ingredients in a small bowl, stirring with a whisk. **3. Combine** brown sugar, ¼ cup butter, and 1 teaspoon vanilla in a large bowl; beat with a mixer at medium speed until blended. Add eggs, 1 at a time, to sugar mixture; beat well after each addition. Add pumpkin; beat well. Fold in flour mixture. Spread batter into a 13 x 9–inch metal baking pan coated with cooking spray. Bake at 350° for 25 minutes or until a wooden pick inserted in center comes out clean. Cool completely in pan on a wire rack. **4. To prepare frosting,** combine 2 tablespoons butter, ½ teaspoon vanilla, and cream cheese in a medium bowl; beat with a mixer at medium speed until blended. Gradually add powdered sugar, beating well. Spread frosting evenly over top of cake. **Yield:** 24 servings (serving size: 1 piece).

CALORIES 188; FAT 5.5g (sat 3.4g, mono 0.9g, poly 0.2g); PROTEIN 3g; CARB 32.5g; FIBER 1g; CHOL 32mg; IRON 1mg; SODIUM 138mg; CALC 51mg

Chocolate Zucchini Cake

Freshly grated zucchini helps make this rich cake moist. When you're testing the cake for doneness, insert the wooden pick in several different places. You may hit a melted chocolate chip the first time, which might make you think the cake isn't done even if it is.

Young Chefs can:

- Measure shredded zucchini and chocolate chips
- Add zucchini and chocolate chips to batter

Older Chefs can:

- Help shred zucchini
- Prepare glaze, and drizzle over cake

CAKE:

Cooking spray
1   tablespoon all-purpose flour
¾   cup granulated sugar
½   cup packed brown sugar
½   cup (4 ounces) ⅓-less-fat cream cheese, softened
⅓   cup vegetable oil
2   large eggs
2   large egg whites
1   teaspoon vanilla extract
11.25 ounces all-purpose flour (about 2½ cups)
½   cup unsweetened cocoa
2   teaspoons baking powder
½   teaspoon baking soda
½   teaspoon salt
½   teaspoon ground cinnamon
¾   cup nonfat buttermilk
2   cups shredded zucchini (about 2 medium)
⅔   cup semisweet chocolate chips

GLAZE:

¾   cup powdered sugar
3   tablespoons unsweetened cocoa
8   teaspoons fat-free milk
2   tablespoons semisweet chocolate chips
½   teaspoon vanilla extract

1. Preheat oven to 350°. **2. To prepare cake,** coat a 12-cup Bundt pan with cooking spray; dust pan with 1 tablespoon flour. **3. Place** granulated sugar and next 3 ingredients in a large bowl, and beat with a mixer at medium speed until well blended (about 5 minutes). Add eggs and egg whites, 1 at a time, beating well after each addition. Beat in 1 teaspoon vanilla. **4. Weigh** or lightly spoon 11.25 ounces flour (about 2½ cups) into dry measuring cups; level with a knife. Combine flour and next 5 ingredients in a medium bowl, stirring with a whisk. **5. Add** flour mixture and buttermilk alternately to sugar mixture, beginning and ending with flour mixture. Stir in zucchini and chocolate chips. Pour batter into prepared pan. Bake at 350° for 1 hour or until a long wooden pick inserted in cake comes out clean. Cool pan on a wire rack 10 minutes. Remove cake from pan; cool completely on wire rack. **6. To prepare glaze,** combine ¾ cup powdered sugar and 3 tablespoons cocoa in a small bowl; stir with a whisk. Combine milk, 2 tablespoons chocolate chips, and ½ teaspoon vanilla in a 1-cup glass measure. Microwave at HIGH 30 seconds or until chocolate melts. Combine powdered sugar mixture with chocolate mixture, stirring with a whisk. Drizzle glaze over cake. **Yield:** 16 servings (serving size: 1 slice).

CALORIES 290; FAT 9.9g (sat 3.2g, mono 3.1g, poly 2.3g); PROTEIN 5.8g; CARB 46.4g; FIBER 1.9g; CHOL 32mg; IRON 1.9mg; SODIUM 226mg; CALC 71mg

Lemon Angel Food Cupcakes

Sifting the flour mixture thoroughly three times incorporates the powdered sugar for a light, tender cupcake. This also allows multiple kitchen helpers to give sifting a try. To help with cleanup, place a kitchen towel underneath the sifter and mixing bowl; shake off any mess into the sink or trash can when you're done.

Young Chefs can:

- Place liners in muffin cups
- Help sift flour mixture

Older Chefs can:

- Add sugar slowly to egg whites
- Spread frosting over each cupcake

CUPCAKES:

2	ounces cake flour (about ½ cup)
¾	cup powdered sugar
¾	cup egg whites (about 5 large eggs)
¾	teaspoon cream of tartar
⅛	teaspoon salt
½	cup granulated sugar
½	teaspoon vanilla extract
2	teaspoons grated lemon rind

FROSTING:

¼	cup butter, softened
2	cups powdered sugar
1	tablespoon 1% low-fat milk
2	tablespoons freshly squeezed lemon juice

Fresh raspberries (optional)

1. Preheat oven to 350°. **2. Place** 16 paper muffin cup liners in muffin cups. Set aside. **3. Weigh** or lightly spoon cake flour into a dry measuring cup; level with a knife. Sift together flour and ¾ cup powdered sugar into a medium bowl; repeat procedure twice. **4. Beat** egg whites, cream of tartar, and salt with a mixer at high speed until frothy. Add ½ cup granulated sugar, 1 tablespoon at a time, beating until stiff peaks form.

Sprinkle flour mixture over egg white mixture, ¼ cup at a time; fold in after each addition. Fold in vanilla and rind. Divide batter evenly among prepared muffin cups. **5. Bake** at 350° for 18 minutes or until lightly browned. Remove from pan; cool completely on a wire rack. **6. To prepare frosting,** beat butter with a mixer at high speed until fluffy. Gradually add 2 cups powdered sugar, beating at low speed just until blended. Add milk and lemon juice; beat until spreading consistency. Spread 2 tablespoons lemon frosting over each cupcake. Garnish with fresh raspberries, if desired. **Yield:** 16 servings (serving size: 1 cupcake).

CALORIES 150; FAT 3g (sat 1.8g, mono 0.8g, poly 0.1g); PROTEIN 1.6g; CARB 30.1g; FIBER 0.1g; CHOL 8mg; IRON 0.3mg; SODIUM 58mg; CALC 4mg

kids taste-testing panel

To help ensure that this book was truly kid-approved, we recruited a variety of kids ages 3 to 12 to taste the recipes and tell us what they thought—and they were brutally honest. If most of the kids didn't like a recipe, it didn't make the cut. We'd like to thank them, as well as their parents, for their participation in the book and for providing us with invaluable feedback.

Anna

Ashley

Julia

Piper

Anna

Nathan

Hannah

Emmie

Cole

Walker

Mary Douglas

Sutton

Stephen

Alora

Cameron

Jarret

Ella

Adeline

Parker

Not Pictured: Tyler

seasonal produce guide

When you use fresh fruits, vegetables, and herbs, you don't have to do much to make them taste great. Although many of these produce items are available year-round, you'll get better flavor and prices when you buy what's in season. The Seasonal Produce Guide below helps you choose the best items so you can create sensational meals all year long.

spring

Fruits
Bananas
Blood oranges
Coconuts
Grapefruit
Kiwifruit
Lemons
Limes
Mangoes
Navel oranges
Papayas
Passion fruit
Pineapples
Strawberries
Tangerines
Valencia oranges

Vegetables
Artichokes
Arugula
Asparagus
Avocados
Baby leeks
Beets
Belgian endive

Broccoli
Cauliflower
Dandelion greens
Fava beans
Green onions
Green peas
Kale
Lettuce
Mushrooms
Radishes
Red potatoes
Rhubarb
Snap beans
Snow peas
Spinach
Sugar snap peas
Sweet onions
Swiss chard

Herbs
Chives
Dill
Garlic chives
Lemongrass
Mint
Parsley
Thyme

summer

Fruits
Blackberries
Blueberries
Boysenberries
Cantaloupes
Casaba melons
Cherries
Crenshaw melons
Grapes
Guava
Honeydew melons
Mangoes
Nectarines
Papayas
Peaches
Plums
Raspberries
Strawberries
Watermelons

Vegetables
Avocados
Beets
Bell peppers
Cabbage

Carrots
Celery
Chili peppers
Collards
Corn
Cucumbers
Eggplant
Green beans
Jicama
Lima beans
Okra
Pattypan squash
Peas
Radicchio
Radishes
Summer squash
Tomatoes

Herbs
Basil
Bay leaves
Borage
Chives
Cilantro
Dill
Lavender
Lemon balm
Marjoram
Mint
Oregano
Rosemary
Sage
Summer savory
Tarragon
Thyme

autumn

Fruits
Apples
Cranberries
Figs
Grapes
Pears

Persimmons
Pomegranates
Quinces

Vegetables
Belgian endive
Bell peppers
Broccoli
Brussels sprouts
Cabbage
Cauliflower
Eggplant
Escarole
Fennel
Frisée
Leeks
Mushrooms
Parsnips
Pumpkins
Red potatoes
Rutabagas
Shallots
Sweet potatoes
Winter squash
Yukon gold potatoes

Herbs
Basil
Bay leaves
Parsley
Rosemary
Sage
Tarragon
Thyme

winter

Fruits
Apples
Blood oranges
Cranberries
Grapefruit
Kiwifruit
Kumquats

Lemons
Limes
Mandarin oranges
Navel oranges
Pears
Persimmons
Pomegranates
Pomelos
Quinces
Tangelos
Tangerines

Vegetables
Baby turnips
Beets
Belgian endive
Brussels sprouts
Celery root
Chili peppers
Dried beans
Escarole
Fennel
Frisée
Jerusalem artichokes
Kale
Leeks
Mushrooms
Parsnips
Potatoes
Rutabagas
Sweet potatoes
Turnips
Watercress
Winter squash

Herbs
Bay leaves
Chives
Parsley
Rosemary
Sage
Thyme

nutritional analysis
How to use it and why

While *The Ultimate Kid-Approved Cookbook* is about feeding your children, many of the recipes are designed for the whole family to enjoy. With this in mind, we've included a full nutritional analysis at the end of each recipe. With chefs, registered dietitians, home economists, and a computer system that analyzes every ingredient we use, *Cooking Light* gives you authoritative dietary detail. We go to such lengths so you can see how our recipes fit into your healthful eating plan.

Here's a helpful guide to put our nutritional analysis numbers into perspective. Remember, one size doesn't fit all, so take your lifestyle, age, and circumstances into consideration when determining your nutrition needs. For example, pregnant or breast-feeding women need more protein, calories, and calcium. And women older than 50 need 1,200mg of calcium daily, which is 200mg more than the amount recommended for younger women. For more information about nutrition guidelines for your children, refer to the information starting on page 10. Go to ChooseMyPlate.gov for individualized plans for you and your children.

In our nutritional analysis, we use these abbreviations

sat	saturated fat	**CHOL**	cholesterol
mono	monounsaturated fat	**CALC**	calcium
poly	polyunsaturated fat	**g**	gram
CARB	carbohydrates	**mg**	milligram

Daily nutrition guide

	Women Ages 25 to 50	Women over 50	Men over 24
Calories	2,000	2,000 or less	2,700
Protein	50g	50g or less	63g
Fat	65g or less	65g or less	88g or less
Saturated Fat	20g or less	20g or less	27g or less
Carbohydrates	304g	304g	410g
Fiber	25g to 35g	25g to 35g	25g to 35g
Cholesterol	300mg or less	300mg or less	300mg or less
Iron	18mg	8mg	8mg
Sodium	2,300mg or less	1,500mg or less	2,300mg or less
Calcium	1,000mg	1,200mg	1,000mg

The nutritional values used in our calculations come from either The Food Processor, Version 8.9 (ESHA Research), or are provided by food manufacturers.

metric equivalents

The information in the following charts is provided to help cooks outside the United States successfully use the recipes in this book. All equivalents are approximate.

Cooking/oven temperatures

	Fahrenheit	Celsius	Gas Mark
Freeze Water	32° F	0° C	
Room Temp.	68° F	20° C	
Boil Water	212° F	100° C	
Bake	325° F	160° C	3
	350° F	180° C	4
	375° F	190° C	5
	400° F	200° C	6
	425° F	220° C	7
	450° F	230° C	8
Broil			Grill

Liquid ingredients by volume

¼ tsp	=	1 ml				
½ tsp	=	2 ml				
1 tsp	=	5 ml				
3 tsp	=	1 tbl	=	½ fl oz	=	15 ml
2 tbls	=	⅛ cup	=	1 fl oz	=	30 ml
4 tbls	=	¼ cup	=	2 fl oz	=	60 ml
5⅓ tbls	=	⅓ cup	=	3 fl oz	=	80 ml
8 tbls	=	½ cup	=	4 fl oz	=	120 ml
10⅔ tbls	=	⅔ cup	=	5 fl oz	=	160 ml
12 tbls	=	¾ cup	=	6 fl oz	=	180 ml
16 tbls	=	1 cup	=	8 fl oz	=	240 ml
1 pt	=	2 cups	=	16 fl oz	=	480 ml
1 qt	=	4 cups	=	32 fl oz	=	960 ml
				33 fl oz	=	1000 ml = 1 l

Dry ingredients by weight

To convert ounces to grams, multiply the number of ounces by 30.

1 oz	=	¹⁄₁₆ lb	=	30 g
4 oz	=	¼ lb	=	120 g
8 oz	=	½ lb	=	240 g
12 oz	=	¾ lb	=	360 g
16 oz	=	1 lb	=	480 g

Length

To convert inches to centimeters, multiply the number of inches by 2.5.

1 in	=					2.5 cm	
6 in	=	½ ft			=	15 cm	
12 in	=	1 ft			=	30 cm	
36 in	=	3 ft	=	1 yd	=	90 cm	
40 in	=					100 cm	= 1m

Equivalents for different types of ingredients

Standard Cup	Fine Powder (ex. flour)	Grain (ex. rice)	Granular (ex. sugar)	Liquid Solids (ex. butter)	Liquid (ex. milk)
1	140 g	150 g	190 g	200 g	240 ml
¾	105 g	113 g	143 g	150 g	180 ml
⅔	93 g	100 g	125 g	133 g	160 ml
½	70 g	75 g	95 g	100 g	120 ml
⅓	47 g	50 g	63 g	67 g	80 ml
¼	35 g	38 g	48 g	50 g	60 ml
⅛	18 g	19 g	24 g	25 g	30 ml

recipe index

subject index